GW00731349

"I was amazed at how engaged the kids were. They were engrossed!"
-Darrin Pearson
Teacher, Coach

If your challenges...
-Keeping students motivated
-Emphasizing the importance of education
-Encouraging students to make wise choices
-Increasing the number of students who graduate successfully

Joseph can help you address these challenges by:
-Inspiring students to pursue their dreams despite obstacles and challenges.
-Demonstrating the importance of education and perseverance in life through his personal testimony.
-Engaging students in humorous role-play and dialogue used to teach valuable lessons to help them succeed in school and in life.
-Providing practical information on how to keep kids motivated, inspired, and engaged in school.

Creative

Inspirational

Life Changing

Fun

To book Joseph for workshops, assemblies, and conferences:
josephmathews.com
josephmathews40@yahoo.com
202-702-5262

Customized
Joseph's presentations are customized to address unique challenges and maximize opportunities.

Unique
Joseph uses a unique approach of interweaving monologues, role-play, motivational testimony, and audience participation to teach lessons, inspire hope, and engender change in students and teachers alike.

Humorous
Joseph is known for making students laugh while making them think critically about their purpose, evaluate their circumstances, and aspire to reach for their wildest dreams.

Personal
As a former high school dropout, Joseph understands the importance of never giving up. Through sharing personal experiences and testimony Joseph lets students know that he can relate to the challenges they face and wants to help them succeed in life.

Special Thanks

To anyone who has ever lay in the bed
at night and dreamt about their lives.
I dedicate this book to you.

To my mother who encouraged me never to
give up during the tough times and to
Willie who provided the light that I
needed to find my way to manhood. I
say thank you and I love you.

And special thanks to my three girls
who put up with me at home — Inaya
Freedom, Journey Crystal, and their
mother and my wife Ronneal Mathews.
You all give me inspiration and make my
life livable. I love you.

The

Dropout

Joseph Mathews

For Joey and Chris...

Part I

Introduction

Like many of the youth growing up in this country I have lived a rough life. At a very young age I was forced to experience many cruel realities and heartbreaking setbacks. With the recent crisis in the middle school, high school, and even elementary school dropout rates, I feel compelled to share my story. Through this book I tell my life story and reveal the happy, sad, and tragic events that contributed to the making of me – "the dropout."

I truly understand the pain of kids who have dropped out of school or who have contemplated dropping out. My experiences have given me a unique insight into the making of a dropout. Dropouts are usually not "bad kids" – or at least they don't start out that way. Dropouts are not born, they're made.

From my very early years, starting in 3rd grade, I was being set up to be a dropout. I know that most teachers work hard and are seeking to enrich the lives of the students they are responsible for. I was unfortunate to encounter some teachers who either didn't care or didn't believe in me. In addition, my parents were overwhelmed and believed that *all* teachers have the best interest of their students at heart. These circumstances laid the foundation for low expectations from teachers and eventually from myself. I was in trouble almost from the very start.

My elementary, middle and high school years were full of more twists, turns and painful losses than some people will experience in their entire lives. It is through these experiences and painful moments that I write this book. I hope it inspires dropouts like me to go back to school and take their dreams and their destinies into their own hands. It is my prayer that youth who have not dropped out will never give up, and keep fighting through all of life's ups and downs.

Believe in yourself and finish the race...

Prologue

The Policeman pulled up to the back door of the jail, pulled me out of the car and walked me inside. No more family no more friends no more football, and no more freedom. My life was over, I had been told many times that this is where I could end up if I didn't change. Never in a million years did I imagine that It would come true.

Chapter 1
History

I was born in a small country town named Bivins. Bivins is a swampy East Texas town right on the border of Texas and Louisiana. Most of the memories I have of my place of birth are filled with my brothers, my cousins, and me racing up and down the dirt road next to our house and playing football in the wide open fields. My house was surrounded by fruit trees, fishing ponds, and the gardens in which we grew our own food.

It wasn't until later on in life that I discovered that the land I was born on and the land that my brothers, my cousins and I ran so freely on was a place that at one time my ancestors wanted to run away from. I was born on a slave plantation. In 1865 when most slaves were being freed, the plantation that my family was enslaved on was given to my grandmother's mother. This land remains in the family to this day.

The Real King of the South

My grandfather was a small man who was known for sitting on his porch telling stories about his life and sharing his wisdom through his singing and guitar playing. His presence in our family is felt strongly even after his death in 1997.

The story of how he ended up in East Texas is as fascinating as he was. When he was 20 years old, he and his 17 year old brother were living in Atlanta, Georgia. This was during a time when Black people were expected to bow down to white people. If they didn't they could be put in jail, or even worse, hung from a tree.

Black men like my grandfather and granduncle were expected to allow white people to run all over them. This reality was accepted by the majority of Black people living in Atlanta during this time.

But my granddaddy wasn't the type of person to let people just run all over him. And one fateful day the course of his life and his future would change forever. I have never known why, but for some reason two white men decided that they wanted to pick on my granduncle. When my grandfather heard about this he decided to pay them a little visit.

When he showed up by himself those two men didn't take him seriously. But by the time it was over both men were lying on the ground sporting multiple knots on their heads and bruised egos to match. Those two men didn't realize that my grandfather was a fighter. Living in the segregated South had forced him to fight for his life everyday.

After giving those two white men a beat down for messing with his brother, his life was in serious danger. It turns out that they were members of the Ku Klux Klan. They wanted revenge but were too embarrassed to admit that they had taken a beating by one young man who was smaller than they were, so they lied and said that they were jumped by my grandfather *and* granduncle. The word traveled fast that the Klan had put a hit out on my granddaddy and granduncle.

And when they returned home they only had a few minutes to grab some money and get out of dodge, because if they didn't act fast they were going to be hanging from a tree by morning. So they sat out on a journey that would change their lives forever.

They hid out in the woods and hitchhiked across the South. My granduncle relocated to Detroit, Michigan where he and much of my family still live today. My grandfather headed towards Texas, the place where he met my grandmother, settled down, and gave birth to a generation of children who gave birth to me, my brothers and all of my cousins.

The Training of a Champion

Every summer most of my cousins came back home and my grandfather put us all to work on the farm milking cows, chopping wood, and plowing the field. Because I was younger than everybody else, I didn't do the heavy work. I did the fishing, and picking food out of the garden.

I especially loved working in the garden because there was a tree that had a wasp nest in it. Every time I went out to the garden, I made the wasps mad by throwing rocks at their nest so they would chase me.

When my father was younger he was a star football player. My mother was a star track runner. Thanks to my parents, I was always more athletic and faster than the average person. Running away from a swarm of angry red wasps was such an adrenaline rush. It felt like I was running for my life. I had no way of knowing that I was practicing for a childhood that would also be filled with running for my life.

My favorite part of the day was when it was time to catch the chickens for dinner. I was always the first one waiting to get into the chicken cage. I always found the chickens more challenging than the wasps, because the wasps only chased me so far but if they couldn't catch me they stopped.

The chickens were a different story. You see, *I* had to try to catch *them*. The first few times I got into the chicken cage was a disaster. Those chickens flat out embarrassed me. I was the fastest cousin. I was able to outrun a swarm of angry red wasps but I was being made to look like a fool by some chickens.

Every day at the same time my grandfather would ask: "Who wants to go into the chicken coop?" I would always be the first one at the gate. Everyday my cousins got a good laugh watching me chase after those chickens, especially when they saw one run right past me making me look foolish, but to me it had become personal. It was now a serious competition. There would be times that we would be starving to eat but in order for us to do so, I would have to work as hard as I could to catch a chicken. To my cousins, those elusive chickens running around were just a game but to me it was about survival.

Being able to outrun the wasps had been like a challenge to me. Outrunning them made me feel like I was the champion of the world, but those chickens taught me a different lesson. They taught me that a real champion is not just someone who has the ability to run away from something. A true champion is someone who has the ability to rise to the challenge and chase down what they want. That was a quality that I would depend on later in life when I saw my dreams running away from me.

I remember one of my older cousins who was visiting from Detroit asking my grandfather why we didn't just go get everything we needed from the store. My grandfather said something that stayed with me for the rest of my life. He told my cousin, "If you're hungry you shouldn't depend on other people to feed and take care of you. That gives them power over your life. The only way that you can truly control your own life is to plant seeds and watch the things you worked hard for grow."

This statement had a profound impact on my life. Even now, I remember this and I use it everyday. The lessons on my family farm are tools that I have used throughout my life.

Moms and Pops

My mother was born and raised on the Southeastern side of Oklahoma in a town named Idabel which is nationally known for its track programs. Idabel has produced more state championships than any other high school program in the country. My mother was a product of this great tradition and was one of the best runners and basketball players to ever come from the town.

Idabel is located in the part of Oklahoma called the Choctaw Nation because its inhabitants were members of one of the Five Civilized Tribes called the Choctaw Indians.

I don't remember much about my mother's mother. I was only 8 years old when she died. The only thing that I remember is that she was a proud Native American woman.

My daddy is a tall, very dark skinned, muscular man. As a young man he volunteered to fight in the Vietnam War. When he returned home he volunteered to go back and fight again. He grew up in East Texas and was a star athlete. I can't tell you how many stories I've heard about how great my daddy was at football. He was known all over the great state of Texas.

My parents met and married in East Texas, and that is where my two brothers, Anthony and Eddie Jr., and I were born. Life was good for our little family in the early years. We started out living a simple life in the country. It's amazing how your life can change over night. I still remember the night that my life changed forever.

Rainy Day and a One Way Ticket

As a kid, spring was my favorite time of the year. The constant tapping of the rain as it hit our metal roof would always put me to sleep. As a child, I always imagined that the rain was tears being shed by God and the angels in heaven because they were sad for the hurting children here on earth. I didn't know that I to would one day be forced to feel and see that same pain and shed tears like the ones that came from heaven.

It turns out that while I was running around living a care free, drama free life, my mother and father's life together was filled with turmoil. I've asked my mother and my older brothers on several occasions to tell me what actually went down between them. I have never been able to get them to tell me.

I believe it's because I am the youngest child and wasn't exposed to the fights and arguments like my brothers. They wanted to protect me, so I'd be lying if I said I know exactly what happened.

Whatever happened, it was so bad that one day my mother picked my brothers up from school and got dropped off at the Greyhound Station. Then she called my daddy to tell him that she was leaving. I was with him and she pleaded with him to bring me to the station but told him that she would have no choice but to leave without me if he was not willing to do so. My daddy loaded me into the car and began driving down a long dirt road.

The smell of rain flowed through the vents and filled the inside of the car. Outside, the wind blew the trees back and forth and drops of rain fell down on the car hitting the windshield so hard that the wipers on the car were barely able to keep up. I remember feeling like something was wrong with him as we drove down the muddy road. I had no clue what was going on. I was just riding and looking out of the window at the rain.

After riding around for awhile, my daddy pulled into the Greyhound Station in a town in East Texas named Atlanta. Standing there in the rain was my mama and my brothers. My daddy helped me out of the car, walked me over to my mama, and then walked away.

My mother had no money and no credit cards, but by faith she walked over to the bus driver with tears in her eyes and asked him if we could get on the bus. The driver looked down at me and my brothers and saw that we were cold, dripping wet and crying. He didn't have the heart to say no, so he let us on the bus.

As the bus pulled off with me and my new family on board I remember looking out of the window at the rain. I often think about how my grandfather left Atlanta, Georgia to start a new life. It's ironic that we left from another place named Atlanta – Atlanta, TX - to start a new life.

I have often thought about that night and how I didn't know at the time that this stormy night was the beginning of a young life that would be constantly filled with storms. Little did I know that the simple life I had once lived would no longer exist, and the new life we were about to embark upon was going to be a living hell. We were on a bus with nowhere to stay, no money, and a one-way free ride to Oklahoma City.

Chapter 2
Geography

We reached Oklahoma City the next morning. I don't know how my mama did it, but she convinced a landlord to give us a place to stay. It was a small one bedroom apartment in a low income housing project on the Northeast side of inner city Oklahoma City. The neighborhood was located right across the street from the Oklahoma State Capitol.

Oklahoma City was unlike anything I had ever seen in my life. People were walking around everywhere and at night the big buildings lit up the sky. I always looked across the way and thought about all of the people in those big buildings and wondered what they did. I thought they must be very rich and very important.

The lights from the buildings reminded me of when I was back on the farm in East Texas and how at night I often looked at the stars and wondered what was out there. I remember how, as a kid, I always had dreams that I was standing in front of a podium speaking to large crowds of people.

Throughout my life very few things have ever happened to me that I didn't dream about first. I guess that's why my heart was heavy when my family loaded up on the bus headed to Oklahoma City. I had dreamt that we were about to live a nightmare.

Unwanted House Guests

When we walked into our little one bedroom apartment you would've thought that every roach in the neighborhood was hanging out at our place. They were on the floor, the walls, and the ceiling. To make matters worse, these were bold roaches! Usually when you walk in somewhere and roaches are present they take off running. Not these roaches! These were gangster roaches. We walked in and they didn't even move. They just looked at us and kept walking around. I guess they figured that they had chased off everyone who ever lived in that apartment and we wouldn't last long either.

That first night I positioned myself in between my brothers, thinking that I'd be safe from the roaches because they'd have to crawl over my brothers to get me. I still wore a shirt over my head because if any did crawl on me, I didn't want them to crawl in my ears.

We had no furniture and no blankets. All we had was the clothes on our bodies. That night, my mama, my brothers, and I laid down on that hardwood floor and got our first night of sleep in Oklahoma City, the place we'd begin our new life.

Hunger Pains

To this day I thank God that neither the Department of Human Services nor Child Protective Services ever came and checked on us. If they had, they would have taken me and my brothers away. Not because my mother was abusing us but because we were hungry.

I wonder what it must have felt like being a mother and having to watch your children starve. I can't count the number of times that my brothers and I went to bed hungry.

My mother was always a spiritual woman. At night when I had trouble sleeping because of my empty stomach and the hunger pains she would come over to me and gently lay her hands on my stomach and pray for me and I would fall asleep.

My mother finally found a job at a newspaper warehouse. I'll never forget the first paycheck she got. My brothers and I couldn't wait for her to get home because we knew that she was going to bring something home to eat.

At about 7:00 p.m. we heard the slow creek of her feet climbing the stairs in our apartment building. When she came through the door she had a sack. That sack held the meal that would save our lives for the next couple of years. After she paid the rent for our small, roach infested apartment, she only had a few dollars left. With those few dollars she went to the store and bought a bag of cornmeal, and some salt and pepper.

In another lifetime I believe my mother could have been a great psychologist because when she reached into that bag and pulled out that cornmeal, salt, and pepper, she was able to convince my brothers and me that this was going to be the greatest meal ever. She boiled the corn meal in hot water then poured in salt and pepper for taste. She put that cornmeal in a bowl and that is what we ate for breakfast, lunch and dinner. One good thing I can say about eating corn meal is that once it goes into your stomach it expands and makes you feel full.

One day, a really nice lady from my mama's job invited us to church. This was the church that we grew up in. My mother is still a member there. On Sunday's, me and my brothers would go to church and then come home and pretend like we were having church service. For some reason they always made me be the preacher and they were the people who hollered out "Amen!" every time I shouted something.

I loved the music and the musicians who played the instruments. They were the same age as my brothers so they made playing instruments look cool. Seeing them play reminded me of how my grandfather introduced me to music on his porch. That love for music would one day be the instrument that helped me through a very tough part of my life.

Young Street Hustler

I remember being at church one Sunday thinking about what my grandfather had told us about taking your destiny into your own hands. I was very thankful for the cornmeal we had to eat, but when I walked outside I would see other kids eating things like cookies, chips and sandwiches. I wanted some of that, so I devised a plan.

I noticed that during Sunday school we always learned Bible lessons out of these little booklets. A light bulb went on: "Why don't we take some of these booklets and sell them to the people in our neighborhood?" At first I shared the plan with my brothers and they looked at me like I was crazy. They said, "Man, I ain't taking nothing out of church! God is going to get you, Joseph!"

In my mind I believed God would be happy with me bringing those Bible lessons to people who hadn't been to church. Plus, my stomach was growling and I couldn't shake the image of those other kids sitting on the steps eating chips, cookies, and sandwiches.

So I grabbed a hand full of those little booklets and put them in my pocket, determined to be eating something other than cornmeal on Monday.

When my mother got her job she laid down one very simple instruction for me and my brothers to follow - do not go outside. Because she didn't get home until late in the evening, my brothers and I hadn't even seen the neighborhood we were living in. We just sat around the house all day. To entertain ourselves everyday we wrestled each other.

Sometimes my middle brother, Eddie, Jr., and I would grab a hand full of the rubber bands that my mama brought home from her job and go to war with the gangster roaches. The object of the game was to see how many roaches we could pop with the rubber bands. Looking back, it seems like a crazy game to play, but that's all we had to do. We didn't have toys to play with and we didn't have a television. As crazy as it sounds, I thank God for the rubber bands and the roaches.

Monday morning rolled around and I remember my mother kissing all of us goodbye and telling us to behave while she was gone. As soon as she left I devised my plan. I had 20 booklets. If I could sell every one for a quarter, I would have $5.00 - enough to go across the street to the corner store and buy some food.

My oldest brother Anthony was always left in charge and he always took his job very seriously so I knew I would have to wait for him to take a nap before I snuck out of the apartment. And like clock-work he laid down around noon and started snoring and that was my moment. I grabbed those Bible lessons, unlocked the door, and stepped outside.

I never understood why we weren't allowed to go outside of our apartment in Oklahoma City because my mama always allowed us to go outside to play in East Texas. I soon found out why she didn't want us outside. In East Texas, most of the people around town were either blood relatives or like family to me.   There was a sense of love and community. You felt like you were loved and could trust your neighbors.

But when I walked into the streets of the city for the first time, the way I saw the world changed. It felt like I was in a movie. People were walking around like zombies. The devastating effects of drugs and poverty had broken the spirits of the people in my neighborhood.

My heart was so broken for the people who I saw. There were kids my age and a little bit older just walking around looking sad and mad at the world. I was living in the heart of a broken neighborhood filled with kids who would go on to become some of the most violent criminals, drug dealers and gang members in the city. Seeing all of the people strung out on drugs and kids from broken homes taught me a very tough and valuable lesson at age 6. I learned that this world would eat you up if you let it.

I walked up and down the street going up to homeless people and people who looked like they could use what I was selling. Although my goal had initially been to go out and make some money to get something to eat, when I saw people hurting it broke my heart so much that I ended up wanting to help them more than I wanted to help myself. I started walking up and down the street talking to people about those Bible lessons and giving them to people who I felt were hurting or just sitting around.

Mission Accomplished

I don't know if it was because I was a cute little six year old kid selling those Bible lessons for a quarter or because the people needed something to pick them up, but when I walked up to them and started talking, I saw people smiling who looked like they hadn't smiled in years.

Most of the people who saw what I was doing decided to give me more than the quarter that I was asking for. Many of them gave me fifty and seventy-five cents. Some of them even gave me a dollar. By the time all of my Bible lessons were gone I had about thirteen dollars. All I could think about was those kids sitting on the porch eating those sandwiches, chips, and cookies so I ran across the street to the store on the corner.

When I walked in, it was an amazing sight. There were all kinds of foods in the store. I had never been in a grocery store before because in the country we grew our own food. Even though there was every kind of food that I could think of, I wanted what those other kids were eating. I walked through that store and picked up bread, baloney, mayonnaise and cheese. Then I went to the cookie and chip aisles. After I got everything I wanted, I walked up to the counter and paid for the food. After paying for the food, I saw that I had some money left over. So I ran over and picked up a gallon of ice cream.

When I got back home my brothers were still asleep so I made sandwiches for all of us and put them in the old refrigerator. I knew my brothers wouldn't check there because we were used to not having food it anyway.

When they woke up they were sitting on the floor talking. I wish I could have recorded their faces when I walked in the room with a plate of sandwiches cookies and chips. We had a big party that day. When we finished our feast, I capped off the party by telling them to go look in the freezer. All you could hear throughout that little apartment were screams of "Ice cream! Ice cream!"

I had learned many lessons growing up on the farm in East Texas. The main lesson that I remembered was my granddaddy teaching us that hungry people don't sit around and wait on other people to feed them, and that if you want something you have to go out and chase it down. That day, I learned to chase down survival. My pursuit of survival started that day when I learned how to turn Bible lessons into cookies.

As a kid I was always a very creative and smart person. Living in the country with very little to do forced me to use my creativity. Although I was the youngest of all of my brothers and cousins they always looked to me when they couldn't think of anything else to do, because I had a unique gift of being able to use my mind to make something out of what seemed like nothing.

This gift would prove to be a life saver for me later on in life but not before those same gifts were stripped away by a person I trusted and was supposed to love me.

Chapter 3
Honors Classes

School finally rolled around. I remember anxiously waiting on my mama to get home so I could go get enrolled. From the very beginning, starting with Pre-Kindergarten and Kindergarten I was always in love with school.

Back in East Texas, Pre-K and Kindergarten were so fun to me. Sometimes I might have been unfair to my classmates because I dominated the class discussion. During science class when the teachers held up pictures of different animals I not only knew every animal but I also knew what they liked to eat and where they went in the winter. I guess part of the reason I had so much knowledge about the animals was because I lived with most of them in the country.

The Making of an Intellectual

My granddaddy was an avid reader. He had all kinds of books lying around by famous African American authors and leaders like W.E.B Dubois, one of the co-founders of the National Association for the Advancement of Colored People (N.A.A.C.P.), the oldest civil rights organization. He also had books about Granville T. Williams and Elijah McCoy, two famous African American inventors who invented many of the things that we use today. And then there were his books about famous abolitionist Frederick Douglas, a black man who was born a slave but set himself free by learning how to read and then helped other slaves obtain freedom.

My grandfather told me stories about the Korean War and World War II which he fought in and one of his brothers died in. My daddy told me about how he fought in Vietnam and my grandmother taught me about slavery and politics in this country. My mother and maternal grandmother talked to me about being Native American or "Indian". I can honestly say that because of all of the porch stories and reading lessons beside my grandfather, I was much more advanced than the average kid. When other kids were learning how to pronounce single words I was speaking in full sentences. And when they were learning how to write single letters I was writing paragraphs.

Although I knew that I was far more educationally advanced than my peers in Pre-K and Kindergarten it never went to my head. It actually made me want to help my fellow students. I was a natural born teacher and leader. My Kindergarten teacher observed this early in the school year. I had mastered all of the basics that they were supposed to teach us throughout the year before the year even started. Whenever my teacher assigned us class work I always finished early and sat quietly until one day the teacher asked me if I wanted to walk around and help the rest of the class. And that was the day that becoming a school teacher became my childhood dream.

Going to school in Oklahoma City was very different than my school in East Texas. The classroom that I was in felt more like a jail cell, but I never let that get me down. I was in the first grade, but when I took the state achievement test my teacher told me that I had scored higher than anyone in my school. I was testing on a 7th grade level. Once again, I was the smartest kid and my teacher was allowing me to help my peers.

I was quite the teachers pet. My teachers loved me because I sat in the front row of the class and raised my hand to answer every question. I even asked them questions about different topics and before you knew it the teacher and I would be engaged in a one on one discussion about the Civil War or World War II or about how Oklahoma was originally designated as a place to send newly freed slaves, or how there were Black people who traveled with the Native Americans on the Trail of Tears. No matter what topic was being discussed, I was like a walking history book.

All of the conversations with my grandfather and grandmother as a kid on our farm had prepared me to hold intelligent conversations with my teachers, having to work hard on the farm and chase chickens prepared me to work hard in the classroom, and seeing the people in my projects walking around hurting and living in a state of hopelessness reminded me of the book that I read about Frederick Douglas. I wanted to learn as much as I could so I could return and help to set them free one day.

One of realities of being poor and living in Section 8 housing is that you have to move a lot. By the time I made new friends we'd be packing up to move somewhere else. I can't count the number of times our family moved. We moved so much that I probably attended every Elementary school in the city. The only good thing about our very first move in Oklahoma City was that we got to move away from that roach motel.

Although my home life was very unstable I continued to work hard in school. One of the reasons I worked so hard was because I had nothing else in my life to feel good about. We were dirt poor and everybody knew it. People at church, people at school, even people in our neighborhood knew it, because there were many nights that we had to borrow matches and candles from them because our lights were cut off. We would even have to go over to our neighbor's houses with empty milk jugs and ask them if we could get some water so that we could take baths and have something to drink because our water was cut off. I honestly can't remember a time in my life as a kid that we had all of our utilities on at the same time.

As long as I dwelled on the circumstances that surrounded me I would get down and depressed, but thinking about school and how good I was at it made me feel better. It actually made me feel like I was finally in control of something in my life. I entrenched myself in school and into learning.

When I entered the 2nd grade I felt that the year was going to be a special one. By this time my mother had found a cheap house in a suburban area of Oklahoma City named Midwest City - the place where I got introduced to white people. Although we were still very poor, the school that I would be attending was one of the best elementary schools in one of the top districts in the state.

Midwest City is the home of Tinker Air Force Base, a major military base that people from all over the world move to. Most of the kids that were in my honors classes were kids of captains, lieutenants, wealthy business people, and influential politicians. They had been all over the world and had attended the best schools, so to be in class with them was exciting to me.

Second grade was very fun for me because even though I was one of only a few black kids in my class I made a bunch of new friends. I was even voted the 2nd grade class President.

The teachers saw how smart I was and after looking at my test scores they decided to put me in advanced classes. I loved it because I was finally being challenged. There were times when the teacher would ask a question and no one would answer. She would look over at me and say, "Joseph, aren't you going to take a stab at the question?" This made me feel special because I knew that she thought enough of me to expect me to know the answer.

Whenever I didn't know something she made sure I learned it. My friends and I always had friendly competitions to see who could answer the most questions and get the best grades. I would crush them every time, after all, I was still the smartest kid in the class. But after the spanking I gave them we would go hang out together at recess and talk about our school work and science projects.

I finally felt like I had found my place, but that summer my mother informed me that once again we would have to move, and once again I would be changing schools.

Chapter 4
Special Ed

Our family had been through so much. My mother worked so hard to take care of us. She did her best to keep our lives stable. I know how much it must have hurt her to see us have to move all of the time and make new friends. I had become so used to moving that it just felt like a normal part of life. I excelled at every school that I had attended, and so far, all of my teachers loved having me in class.

We moved a couple of miles away in another low income Section 8 house. The school that I was transferred to was in the same district as the other one and as far as academics were concerned, the students performed on the same level as the students at my old school.

Up to this point everybody in my life saw that I was born with a special gift and wanted to nurture it. They allowed me to help my peers and let me take the lead in class discussions on a variety of topics. So it was very natural for me at the age of 8 to trust that my new teacher and my new school would see my potential and do the same. I was in for an awfully rude awakening. This was the beginning of the end for me.

The Murder of an Intellectual

My mama walked me to the bus stop, kissed me goodbye, and I was off to my new school. When I got there I didn't know anybody, but that was okay because I was used to making new friends. I was talking to everybody and anybody I saw. I found my class and walked in with a big smile. My teacher was sitting in the chair at her desk. When she saw me she just looked at me - no words, no smile, just a blank stare. But I was a nice and happy kid so I went over and introduced myself. At the time I didn't think much about her not saying anything to me, until I watched her walk over and greet all of the other kids that were coming in. Then I realized that the half smile she had given me was fake.

Every school I had ever gone to I sat on the front row as close to the teacher as I could. I wanted to be close so I could answer and ask as many questions as I could.

When the bell rang, all of the kids began to sit down. I put my things in a desk on the front row and walked over to my chair. When I sat down the teacher looked at me and stood up. She looked at the whole class then focused on me and said that she had already arranged a seating chart. I had been around other very smart kids before so I knew that the other kids that were sitting beside me were sitting there for the same reason that I was.

By the time the teacher finished moving us around, all of them were still on the front row. They had just been moved one seat over. I, on the other hand, ended up being moved to the very back corner of the class, as far away from her desk as I could get.

I was not happy at all with this new arrangement because I knew this would make it difficult for me to really answer and discuss questions the way I used to at my other schools. Sitting in the back would make it almost impossible to compete with the kids who were sitting in the front of the class.

I raised my hand and when she walked over I politely asked her if I could move closer to the front. She gave me that fake smile again and said, "If I let you move I'll have to let everybody else move." So there I was sitting in the back over in a corner on the first day of class of my 3rd grade year.

I had been through a lot in my short life so being put at the back of class was something that was very hurtful to me. Fortunately, I was always a very optimistic kid. Because I just knew when we started doing work and having class discussions she would finally see how smart I was and how good I was at helping other people with their work, and she would be compelled to move me to the front of the class.

I soon found out that she had no intention of letting me move to the front of class. Putting me back there had nothing to do with her seating arrangements at all. Putting me in the back was symbolic of what she thought of me as a person and as a student. I was 8 years old and about to learn one of lifes harshest realities and that was that people treat you the way they view you.

All of my previous teachers, most of whom were white, had always treated me like I was a good kid. They knew that I was a smart leader and I knew that when they looked at me I was loved by them, but this teacher didn't see a smart, nice country kid who was full of a love for learning and teaching. She looked at me and saw a poor, dumb, and dirty ghetto kid, and that's how she treated me.

It was one thing for me to be seated in the back of classroom, but when we started having discussions and doing class work she wouldn't call on me when I raised my hand. It was devastating. She would be teaching and when she stopped to ask the class a question I usually knew the answer. I would raise my hand up high almost standing up burning to answer the questions but when she saw that I was the only one with my hand up she would answer the question herself and move on.

This went on for a few days until I couldn't contain my self anymore. I was so upset about not being called on in class anymore that one day she asked the class a question about a math problem and no one else knew the answer so I just ignored her rule of raising your hand before you speak and yelled out the answer. I took a gamble by answering the question because I wanted so much to show her that I was smart. I knew that I would have to pay the consequences for speaking without raising my hand, but she hadn't been calling on me so I took the gamble. It didn't pay off. Instead of telling me "good job" or giving me a warning, she fussed at me and made me turn my desk around. Now, everyday when I came to school I had to sit in the back of the classroom with my desk turned around.

Guilty Until Proven Innocent

Every Friday was popcorn day. Popcorn was 50 cents. Most of the time my mother wouldn't have any money to give me but one Friday she gave me the money to buy popcorn. At the end lunch one of the girls in my class put her money in her desk, and someone stole it. When I walked up to buy my popcorn the teacher asked me to empty my pockets. I took out the money that mama had given me and she gave it to the little girl in front of everybody like I was the one who had stolen her money.

Now, my desk was out in the hallway for the rest of the day while they ate popcorn. I was at a new school where nobody knew me and everybody in my class looked at me like I was a dumb, bad kid. They wouldn't even talk to me, let alone play with me.

Probably the hardest thing for me to deal with was the day she picked kids to be the class helpers. I wanted to cry because I was always the kid who finished his work first and got to help the other kids. Now, I was isolated from the rest of the class like I was in jail. No more friends, no more answering questions, and no more helping my peers. I couldn't even turn around and look as the helpers walked around and helped the kids but I knew the kids that she picked and knew I was smarter than all of them.

Sitting in the back of the classroom and not being allowed to participate in class opened the door for me to start thinking about all of the bad things that had happened in my life. Not having a daddy around, not having anything to eat and moving from project to project made me feel like there was no hope for poor Black kids because the only thing that I had ever seen was poor Black kids. Thinking about this made me very angry and defiant.

The teacher never came to the back of the classroom. The class helpers came to the back but that was even harder because I knew I was supposed to be doing what they were doing. I became so angry that I just stopped doing my work all together. Everyday I came and sat at my desk doing nothing. My spirits were falling further and further down. And then it happened...

Special Ed:
The Miseducation of Me

One month into the school year I showed up and my teacher told me that I was being moved to another classroom. At first I was fine with the move because anything other than that corner was fine for me; but when I walked into my new classroom I realized that something wasn't right. I looked around and very quickly noticed that most of the kids that were in my new class were mentally handicapped and much younger than I was. They were doing work that I had done in Pre-K in East Texas and I was given the same assignments that everyone else was given.

I pointed out to the teacher that we all had the same work and she told me to sit down and be quiet. I had been placed in a self contained Special Education classroom, and this is where I would spend the rest of the school year – all day, every day - just rotting away in this room.

From the time I left East Texas I'd remained strong. We had slept on hardwood floors with roaches, had no food to eat, and we spent many nights in the dark, but I never shed a single tear. I guess because school gave me an outlet to mend my broken heart. The day I realized that the only thing I had going for myself and the only thing I knew that would get me out of the ghetto was being taken away from me I broke down and cried right in the middle of that classroom. I remember crying and thinking about all of those nice teachers that had looked at me with love in their eyes. I wished that one of them would come and save me and tell them that they were wrong about me, but no one ever came.

I thought about all of my friends at my old school and how we used to compete and wondered what they were doing. I wished I could be with them again. In less than one year I went from honors classes to Special Education classes. For the rest of the year I watched myself turn into one of those lifeless, hurting, and mad at the world kids that I saw walking around my projects looking like half dead zombies. And that's how I felt, - like a zombie because the day I was put in that class all of the wounds from

my past were ripped open and a part of me
died instantly.

Chapter 5
Anger Mismanagement

Third Grade was a tough year. To make matters worse after being mislabeled and mistreated I was held back that year as well. The year of Special Education completely broke my sprits. I honestly believe there is nothing worse than for a youth to be gifted with an amazing ability to fly, and not being given the opportunity to do so, because someone else has decided that they belong in a cage.

That's what happened to me I was 8 years old when that school clipped my wings so that I couldn't fly and that created an internal conflict inside of me that would change my life forever. No matter who you are, no one can be caged up like an animal psychologically without eventually physically acting out like an animal. I began to feel as if my life was of no value to other people and therefore it was no longer of value to me. There is nothing more dangerous than a kid who no longer values his life.

Playground Boxing Champ

Before I continue, I must say that out of all of the things I did as a kid, this point in my life is one of the times I wish I could take back the most.

Remember, I was the son of parents who were extremely athletic so all of my life I was very muscular and strong. Being muscular, strong, and *angry* proved to be a bad thing for the other kids on the playground for the next couple of years. I beat up a lot of people. The only time I wasn't in a fight was when I was suspended from school for fighting or in juvenile detention for stealing from some store.

I'm so glad that they didn't have *YouTube* when I was a kid because I used to beat kids up so often that people would probably be watching my fights and it calling it "Josephs Greatest Knock-Outs."

Not a day has gone by that I haven't wished I could go and find every person that I ever beat up and tell them that I'm sorry. I once heard a quote which states "hurt people, hurt people". This statement describes me perfectly. I was hurting people because I was hurting and I felt like I had no way to express my pain other than combat.

Often, when I was disruptive, my teacher put me in the hallway. When I was out there my mind would start to drift. All of the good memories of my simple life on the family farm were long gone. I felt like I was an old man now. Many times I thought about my life in East Texas and how things seemed so much more innocent back then. Then I would just cry. I missed being with my grandfather, I missed being with my teachers and friends at my old school who loved me. I wondered what they were doing and if they ever thought of me, or for that matter, if they remembered me.

Most of the time when I was in the hallway by myself I thought about the dreams I had in East Texas about speaking to crowds of people. As suddenly as those memories came to me they left, because I was no longer the nice loving kid that I used to be. I was no longer the kid who loved school and loved everybody. Now, I hated everything about school and I even hated myself. Even though all of my teachers who'd treated me with love were white, my 3rd grade teacher made me angry, hateful and distrustful of all white people.

Chapter 6
Athletics

The years of being treated like I wasn't capable of learning was taking its toll on me. By 6th grade year I had so much anger built up inside of me that I was a time bomb waiting to explode. I had earned a notorious reputation for being a bully. I didn't get to participate in activities at school anymore because my grades were so bad and I was always in trouble.

One day my teacher let me go to gym. Mr. Porter, the first Black man I'd ever seen in a school was the gym teacher. When I entered the gym there was a mat lying out on the floor. I asked "What is that?"

He responded, "That's a wrestling mat, do you want to try it out?"

I wanted to try it so I walked onto the mat, not knowing that I was walking onto something that would later help save my life. The concept of wrestling just seemed to click. The objective was simple; grab your opponents, take them down to the ground, and pin them if you can. So I joined the wrestling team.

King of the Mat and the Track

Mr. Porter told me that I would be wrestling kids my size. That seemed too easy because I used to wrestle my older brothers all of the time. The stakes were much higher with them because they were bigger and we didn't just wrestle for fun, we wrestled for food!

Without any experience and with just a few days of practice after school I walked out on the mat for my first match. My opponent didn't know what hit him. I don't think his mother was in the stands because if she had been, she would've come running to his aid. I was like a janitor and he was my mop. I drug him all over the mat and pinned him in the first period.

For the rest of the season I pinned everyone I wrestled and went on to win the All-City Championship. It was the first time I felt good about myself in years. Even more importantly, it was the first time anyone had felt good about me in years so when track season rolled around and Mr. Porter asked me to join the track team I didn't hesitate. I remembered all of those days in East Texas when I used to race my cousins and the wasps. I remembered how my mother was a track star, so I knew that those kids didn't stand a chance against me.

That track season I didn't lose a single race in the 100 or 200 meters. I won All City in track as well. From that day on, when I walked into the school everybody smiled and looked at me with admiration.

The Joseph who was once an honor student had died a long time ago. The attention I once received because I got straight A's was now replaced with being on everybody's watch list because I was viewed as a trouble maker. So naturally, when I started getting attention because I was fast and athletic, I knew that I had something special. Sports were my new ticket. Joseph the athlete had been born and replaced the Joseph who used to get attention for academics.

Part II

Chapter 7
Junior High

By the time that I reached Junior High School, I had accomplished a lot athletically. Track and wrestling had taken me all over the country. I was well known around the city as a great athlete.

Football would take my popularity to a new height. I had never played football before but when I showed up to school the football coaches knew who I was and how fast I was from elementary school. They begged me to come out and play. They were white men and the team was mostly white so I was hesitant, because I had developed a serious distrust for white people but I figured I would give it a try.

On the first day of practice I walked into the locker room. There were two kids sitting close to my locker. I had every intention not to speak to anyone; I was just going to practice. But these guys just continued to bug me and ask me a ton of questions.

The only thing that saved them for being on "Joseph's Greatest Knock-Outs" was the fact that track and wrestling had taught me to control my anger a little. These two guys were determined to be my friends so I said "hello" and we started talking. Their names were Joey and Chris - two blonde haired white kids.

I hadn't trusted a white person in years, but Joey and Chris were different. Their families often invited me over for dinner and always took me out with them like I was part of the family. They reminded me of the friends that I had when I was in the 2nd grade. We ended up being the best of friends.

When I started playing football in Junior High School, my life changed overnight. Some people may know what I'm talking about; however, most people will never know what it's like to be a star athlete. Imagine people doing whatever you want them to do. Imagine people always wanting to get close to you and placing you on a pedestal. Everywhere I went, people knew who I was and wanted to talk to me about sports. I turned into a local celebrity because of football. In fact, most of the people in my life were only there because of football.

It's true that your reputation follows you. Although I was becoming extremely popular and respected because of sports, my high school years would reveal to me that sports would be the only thing I was respected for.

Chapter 8
The Dummy

By the time I reached high school I was one of the most popular athletes in the state. I also started to gain some national attention. I was in the newspaper regularly and the local news stations would show highlights of my touchdown runs on the Friday night high school football round up. But in my heart something was missing.

I was always very aware of things that were going on around me, and I knew that everybody around me except Joey and Chris thought I was a dumb athlete. Many people knew that I was just showing up to school when I felt like it and getting passed on. I remember getting grades for classes that I never showed up for. I had settled into the role as the dumb athlete.

One day our equipment manager stopped me on my way to practice. I was walking out of the locker room and he asked me this simple question: "Is it true?"

"What do you mean?" I replied.

He answered, "Joseph, what are you going to do with your life? I heard that you can't read. Life is going to be hell for you."

To this day, I don't believe he had bad intentions. He was just repeating what he'd heard and what everybody thought about me. I told him that I could read and then he asked me to show him. He went and got one of the player's history books from a locker laid it down on the counter and asked me to read for him. I froze because I hadn't even picked up a book and read since I was in the 2nd grade. He was the first person since then to ask me to.

All of these years, no one had ever even bothered to ask me to read because they didn't think I could. The saddest part of all is that those who didn't think I could read never even bothered to offer to teach me.

I knew that I used to be a great reader but as I stood there frozen I started questioning if I could read. I just closed the book and walked off because I really didn't know if I could read anymore and I was too afraid to try and find out that I couldn't.

I remember thinking about a statistic that I had heard when I was younger. I heard that the government bases how many prisons and jails they are going to build on 3rd grade reading scores. They know that after third grade, success in school is based on the ability to read. Every subject from Math, Science, Social Studies, History, and Geography is based on the ability to read and comprehend. Kids who cannot read get left behind. They get put in the back of the classroom and ignored. And when a kid is ignored, they start to feel like no one cares so they just give up and become angry and defiant. Angry and defiant kids fight, steal, and have no respect for authority. They don't care about rules and not caring about rules leads to kids getting in trouble.

In essence, I learned that the government was building empty prisons because they were waiting on mentally enslaved kids like me to mess up so they could physically enslave me. Right then and there I realized that I wasn't free because I couldn't read. I was a slave. I felt like I was just being used for sports by everybody I knew.

Everyday people looked at me and smiled and I knew that they were not smiling at Joseph, the smart kid who wanted to be a teacher. They were smiling at Joseph, the great dumb athlete who couldn't read. They didn't know the *real* me. I felt really lonely and after this point sports were no longer fun.

Chapter 9
My Boys in the "Hood"

From 7th grade on, Joey and Chris were my best friends. They were the only ones who really knew me. Our friendship was never based on my athleticism. We never even really talked about sports. We always talked about girls, music, and life. They always made me feel like I was smart. That's why I called them my friends.

After awhile though, I started hanging out more with my friends who lived around me in the "hood". We lived in the same neighborhood and in a lot of ways we were living the same lives, so I started to feel closer to and spending more time with them. Although I had been attending a top school across town my family still lived in the "hood".

Murder One

In Oklahoma City, during the 90's, gangs were not just *a* way of life they were *the* way of life. You were either a Blood or a Crip. The neighborhood I was from had developed such a bad reputation for drive by shootings and shoot outs that it was given the nickname "Murder One". It was appropriately named because it was the number one place to get murdered in the Oklahoma City area.

When the Crips and the Bloods hit the city in the late 80's, I was a little kid. The change happened over night. Gang members from California flooded the streets of the city. Then the movie *Colors* came out. After these events, Oklahoma City was never the same.

People who used to be cool with each other become instant enemies because they chose to be affiliated with different gangs. I even saw blood brothers and first cousins murdering one another.

I honestly believe that no other movie has done as much damage to the Black community as *Colors*. Most people from the outside didn't believe that in a city like Oklahoma City, gangs and violence could be so bad. They said, "Man, ain't nothing going on in Oklahoma City", and they were right. There was nothing *constructive* going on, which was the reason we were worse off than many other cities. When that movie was released, kids living in the "hood" had nothing to do and nothing to be apart of so when they were introduced to the Crips and Bloods everybody wanted to be one.

For the most part, I avoided hanging in the streets because I was so busy playing sports, but as I starting spending more time with my friends who were in gangs I got sucked in. A lot of people who visited from out of town said that my homies were "Wanna Be's" but that only made matters worse because now they had something to prove. I witnessed killing after killing of my so-called "enemies" and my so-called "friends".

The city was like a war zone and I was living right in the middle of it. I can't count how many friends I lost in a short period of time. Every time I looked up an innocent person was being shot.

I had a friend named Kim who I ran track with. Her mother always invited me over for dinner because she knew my family didn't have much to eat. Every time I went over there, her mother would talk to us about staying out of trouble, Kim, her brother Jason and her little sister Fredericka, who always stayed out of trouble, were a beautiful family and they had embraced me like a part of their family.

In a two year span, Fredericka and Jason were both dead – both were victims of drive by shootings. To make matters worse, about five years later Kim's mother was killed in a car accident. I believe after seeing two of her three children gunned down she was half dead already.

Chapter 10
New School,
Same Problems

My junior year, I enrolled in a school closer to my house. I had become accustomed to never staying in one place too long anyway. Years of being moved around because of living in Section 8 housing can do that to a kid. I guess I changed schools because I was trying to run away from my past. I hated who I had become, I hated other people, and hated the feeling that I had when people looked at me.

The decision to leave my old school was somewhat difficult; not because I was going to miss my coaches or teachers but because I would miss my friends Joey and Chris. They always had something crazy to say to make me laugh and forget about my problems. Joey was a pretty-boy and always had girl drama. Chris was the school comedian who always made everybody laugh.

Joey and Chris were the only friends I had who knew who I really was, believed in me and loved me even during the times I didn't even love myself. They had given me life, but I walked away from them because I felt like I had nothing to give them in return. I couldn't let go of the demons I was wrestling with so I figured it would be best to just walk away from everybody.

I was only at my new school for a couple of weeks before I started realizing that you can't run away from your problems, especially when you are a part of the problem! I didn't feel any better going to the new school. Actually, I felt worse.

Every day away from my friends, I grew more and more depressed. I was on the verge of doing something to someone or myself. Walking away from Joey and Chris had been the hardest thing for me to do. I hadn't called them or gone to see them since I had left. I heard that they were not taking my leaving well, but I was doing what I felt I needed to do and that was running away from the problems I was having.

I started playing football at my new school to cover up my depression and keep from going crazy. We had a big game coming up against our cross-town rivals on that upcoming Friday. But on that Tuesday before the big game ever came, I would experience one of the most heartbreaking days of my life.

Hard to Say Goodbye

After coming to my new school, I tried to forget the only true friends that I'd ever known and loved. But that Tuesday after school, a boy who knew my friend Chris stopped me and broke the news to me. He told me that Chris had been killed in a car crash during lunch. I cannot explain the pain that I felt. The truth is I was so hurt I couldn't feel anything. I was in complete shock. I couldn't breathe.

The coach asked me to come to practice to take my mind off of the crash. I don't even remember what happen next. I just remember standing outside at football practice completely numb trying to convince myself that this was just a dream. For the first 30 minutes I just stood there at practice in complete astonishment because I had just been told that one of the only two friends I had in the whole world had just died.

As crazy as this may sound, I succeeded in convincing myself that what I just heard about Chris was wrong and that he would be coming by my house checking on me later on that day. That is, until a long line of cars pulled into the parking lot by our practice field. Everybody thought it was the media, but it wasn't. After the news of the crash the coach at my old school decided to cancel practice, so Joey and the rest of the team loaded up in their cars to find me because they knew that I was hurting.

I stood on the field in disbelief. Joey and the whole football team were standing there waiting to console me. That's when I realized that Chris's death was real. The only thing I could think about was his father who treated me like a son, his mother who cooked for me, and his little sister who used to brag on me and Chris down at the Junior High. All I could think about was how hurt they must be right now.

I'd been hurt so many times. Chris and Joey had always been there for me, but after this tragedy I didn't believe in anything anymore. I swore I wouldn't trust anyone else with my heart again.

Chapter 11
Permanent Ditching

After Chris's death, my already unstable life became even more unstable. I started hanging more and more with my friends who had dropped out of school and were now just running the streets. I showed up to school but that was mostly just to kill time. I don't think I even turned in one assignment.

I started contemplating dropping out because I didn't see how school was helping me. Actually, school seemed to be the thing that was hurting me the most. I started thinking about the fact that I probably wouldn't be able to get a good job because I couldn't read. The truth was I didn't really want a job because I saw my homies making money selling drugs. A few weeks after Chris's death I woke up and decided I was not going back to school.

The Dropout

My mother tried to keep me on the right track, but she no longer had control of me. Truthfully, I was no longer in control of myself. I gave all of the power over to every negative thing that had ever shown up in my life. That's what was controlling me. I found out that allowing something or someone else to have control over you can be a very bad and deadly thing.

During my youth in the late 90's, the way to make money was selling drugs, stealing cars, or stealing radios out of cars. Me and my homies tried our hand in all three.

After leaving school I starting living like an animal. I didn't just leave school; I left my mother's house. I was moving from house to house and staying wherever someone would let me lay my head.

The Bike

There was this little kid in my neighborhood. He had a really nice bike. One evening I decided to go take it. I remember seeing him ride into his driveway and get off of his bike to get a drink of water. That was my chance. I ran up and jumped on the bike and started pedaling away as fast as I could.

I looked back and that little kid was chasing after me as fast as he could. He wasn't willing to just let someone get away with something that belonged to him. It was a strange feeling because as he chased me I could see the person I used to be inside of him. I felt kind of sorry for him, but me and my crew had a full fledged hustle going on and he was on our hit list. We took his bike to the pawn shop and sold it. I was on the fast track to nowhere.

Jimmy

The homeboy Jimmy was kind of like me. He had the ability to play sports but he wanted to hang in the streets. Like me, he was never a full fledged gang member; he just hung out with them. He found out that at the end of the day it really doesn't matter if you're in a gang or not, all you have to do is hang with them.

One Sunday night some of the guys who I ran the streets with came over to my homeboy Jimmy's house and asked him if he wanted to roll with them. Knowing Jimmy, he probably didn't want to go but he didn't want them thinking he was soft so he agreed to go.

That was a serious mistake. He jumped in the back seat and they headed toward the other sided of town into rival gang territory. The dudes that Jimmy were with knew what they were about to do, but Jimmy had no clue. They drove through the parking lot of a club where all of the gang members hung out, waited until they got right in the middle of the crowd, and then started throwing up gang signs, and then drove away. During that close brush with death they yelled out of the window, "Just wait right there, we'll be back".

For the life of me, I don't know what my homeboys were thinking. After telling all of those gangsters to wait right there, Jimmy and the homies went back. When they got back, none of the gang members were in the parking lot, so they pulled up and slowly drove through the parking lot again.

All of a sudden, about seven people jumped out from behind cars and surrounded their car. They started shooting and the guys in the front seat were killed instantly. Jimmy wasn't hit; Because He was hiding in the back seat.

Just as the guys who had shot up the car were getting ready to leave the scene, Jimmy crawled out of the car because he thought they had already left. And when he came crawling out of the car the rival gang members saw him and shot him three times in the back. My boy Jimmy died in a pool of blood in the parking lot of that club.

I wonder what was going through Jimmy's mind, when he was being shot at. Was he thinking about his mama or his little brother and how much he would be missed by them if he died? I believe in my heart that right before Jimmy crawled out of the car he cried and prayed for another chance and promised that if he got out of that situation alive, he would change his life. But a person only gets so many chances before the chances run out. Sadly he had been given chance after chance to make a change. As a result of not choosing to do so, his life was tragically ended that night.

Jimmy's death taught me a valuable lesson. And that is if you're hanging with someone and their life is in danger, your life is in danger as well, because bullets don't care if you're innocent.

The Homie Reggie

After Jimmy died, my homeboy Reggie started making a bunch of money selling dope. We started hanging tight. One day we received a supply from one of the main drug dealers in the neighborhood. I was on my way to sell drugs for the first time.

I vividly remember our first time hitting the streets together. We rolled into the projects and I got out of the car. I stood there looking at the people. I noticed them walking around like lifeless zombies, just like the people I used to see when my family and I first moved to Oklahoma City. These people were strung out on drugs, and strung out on hopelessness.

I looked in the eyes of the children and saw that their hearts and spirits had been broken from years of living in the ghetto. These kids didn't have anything to eat just like me when I was their age. They never had a say so about where they were born or who they were born to. These kids were being forced to live around drugs, violence and death. Most of them had been born to crack addicted mothers and had never known their fathers. They were the products of the crack epidemic that had hit my neighborhood in the early 90's, destroying so many people's lives. I wondered if there were any kids living there that were like me when I was their age who dreamed of becoming a teacher one day. Or kids who had a calling on their lives and always had the feeling that they would one day come back and save the people in their community.

I started thinking about how just 10 years earlier I was 6 years old like many of those kids and how I used to walk up and down those same streets selling Bible lessons to the people for food but after seeing how much they were hurting decided to just start giving those lessons away.

Now here I was about to sell drugs to the same people I had once cried for. I decided right then and there that I would not help to create another generation of addicts, killers and broken families. I walked away from that opportunity to make money, Because the drug game wasn't for me. I had to get another hustle.

Chapter 12
Hustling 101

After my experience of almost selling drugs in the projects I started thinking about my life more. I had always been a very observant person so it didn't take much for me to notice that almost every other week one of my friends was getting locked up. My homeboy Reggie's fate wasn't any different. Less than a year later from that day he tried to get me to sell drugs with him he was sentenced to 15 years in our state's Federal Penitentiary where he remains today.

Many more of my friends were not so lucky. I had to attend their funerals. By now

I had been to so many of my friends funerals who had died from violence that no one on this earth could have convinced me that my time wasn't coming soon.

Funeral Competition

Funerals were always a funny thing to me. After one of our friends died, my homeboy's and I would show up and sit toward the back and put our heads down. During the funeral I always glanced over and looked at my dead friend's mother, crying and screaming for her son. The son who she'd loved since giving him life now here she was crying her heart out wishing she could bring him back to life.

During these moments, I thought of my mother and envisioned myself lying in the casket. I thought about how hurt she would be if that were me - her baby boy whose little stomach she used to rub and sing to and dance with.

It was the most interesting thing to me because me and the homies would watch our fallen homeboys mother cry her heart out and then go right back out to the streets and do the same things that had gotten our homeboy killed. It was like we were in a competition to see who could break our mama's heart next.

The thought of dying was never that hard to conceive because I had gotten used to walking around half dead anyway. I guess during this period, the thought of losing my life felt normal because I was already lost.

Booster Club

After being out of school for awhile I devised a plan to move to the next level of hustling. Living life on the streets forces you to either work for or steal the things that you want. I figured out away to do both.

One weekend me and the homies were hanging out at a mall that wasn't too far from my home of the moment. We always hung out at this mall on the weekends. One weekend we were walking by a popular clothing store and one of the homies said, "Man, that place is always packed with people. I bet they make a bunch of money".

Right then, I developed a plan to take the hustle to the next level; I would dive into the crazy world of boosting clothes. But first I would have to get hired. Once that happened I would let my boys come in and steal clothes so we could sell them.

The manager of the store was an attractive young lady and I had never had problems with the girls. Actually, when I was going to school I was a player. I figured that being able to charm this lady into hiring me wouldn't be hard. I was right. I got the job - my first legal job. I was living proof that people can do the right thing for the wrong reasons.

I started working at the store and immediately made it a point to learn how the store was run. I observed the times of the week when the store was busiest and the days when no one came in. I wasn't getting a lot of hours because the other salespeople who were there before me took up all of the hours.

We didn't get paid much so everybody relied on the commission from their sales. I got paid even less because I was the low man on the totem pole, but that was okay. While they were fighting over commission I was developing a plan to make sales on the side. The crazy thing about the situation is that shortly after getting hired I started out-selling all of them. I always excelled at competition and this job was all about competing.

Growing up in the hood, I learned how to talk and listen to people so this job was too easy for me. I even had costumers who would only shop with me. Some of the other salespeople got jealous because my sales were higher than theirs so I started getting scheduled to work on the days that no one came in the store. At first I was mad because I knew they were just hating on me. Then I realized that this was the moment that I'd been waiting for.

After working there for a while the store managers got comfortable with me so they started putting me on the schedule throughout the week. Weekdays were the slowest days of the week and therefore the days no one else really wanted to work. That was fine with me because it would just be the manager and I in the store. I also observed that they didn't take inventory the way they should. The assistant manager lived close to the mall so whenever she could get away with it she went home after she clocked in. That was the opening I had been waiting on and that's also when the trouble started.

I would have my boys come in and act like they were shopping. When they came up to the counter I acted like I was ringing them up. They walked out with clothes which we planned on selling for half the price.

Every week my boys came in the store, filled their bags, and walked out. We were getting paid and the word started getting out that I was the man to get the hook-up on clothes from the mall. One day one of my co-workers walked in on his day off. He'd heard about what I was doing and wanted to get the hook up too. I was hesitant at first because I didn't really know him and plus he was kind of "shifty eyed", but after he kept insisting I gave in and gave him the hook-up too.

For the next couple of weeks he and I took turns coming in on our off days and getting the hook-up. One day when he showed up to work the manager asked him if he had noticed anything suspicious about the clothes from the storage coming up missing. He knew he couldn't just tell on me without getting in trouble too so he said he didn't know what was happening to the clothes.

At that point, he knew he had to develop a plan to get the heat off of himself and onto me. It turns out that before he came to me to get the hook-up he was letting his friends come to the store and do the same thing that my friends were doing. He knew that the manager suspected something so when he found out that I was down he came into the store to set me up.

It was a Wednesday and he was working by himself. I had just worked the day before and he came in and grabbed a lot of new outfits. Something told me there was something shady about this cat but I ignored it. So I walked in and everything seemed cool.   He looked at me and said, "What's up?" so I proceeded to pick out the clothes I wanted. We held a small conversation and then I walked up to the counter with the pair of pants I wanted. As usual, he acted like I paid for them, put them in a bag for me, and I walked out of the store.

It's amazing how most of the time we know when somebody isn't real, or not our true friend but we choose to ignore the signs of their shadiness because we just want someone to hang with. I found out the hard way that it's hard to do dirt with someone who's not dirty.

I walked out of the mall with that bag and as soon as I got to the parking lot, about three mall police officers pulled up, surrounded me, and told me to freeze. He had called the police on me. When they walked me back into the mall in handcuffs and asked him if he wanted to press charges against me, he said, "Yes."

I had just turned 17 and I was on my way to jail.

Chapter 13
Juvenile Detention

The ride to jail was a long one, especially because of how and why I ended up in this position. Getting sent to jail by a person who was just as guilty was a very hard thing to swallow. I hadn't even arrived at the jail house before I started plotting how I was going to get back at my co-worker for selling me out.

It wasn't like I hadn't been in trouble with the law before, but this time I was old enough to go to the adult jail and not just a holding room until my mama came to pick me up. This was it. The orange jump suit they put me in made it feel like the real deal.

The dreams that I had about working to free the lost and hurting people in my old neighborhood as a kid seemed impossible at this point because I was locked up. Man I was a statistic, just like my family members who were slaves on the plantation.

The difference in them and me though was that they had no choice, they were born that way.

But here I was, born free but choosing to live like a slave. This is the point in my life where I had to make some tough decisions because I was 17 years old and sleeping in and adult jail.

Being in jail didn't fully hit me as I walked down the hallway, but when they put me in that cell and the door slammed shut, I almost passed out. I was reminded, once again, of that statistic about the government basing how many prisons and jails they're going to build on 3rd grade reading scores.

Here I was a former straight A student who was in honor classes then got thrown into special education classes where the teachers wouldn't allow me to read anything other than Pre-Kindergarten level books.

The day I was put in the back of the class was the day that my anger, defiance and rebellion started. That was the day that I started being disrespectful to authority and doing all of the things that lead to young people going to jail. It was right in that jail cell that I realized I was a walking future prisoner. This jail had been built for kids like me.

My 3rd grade teacher and that school sat me up for failure, but now that I was a teenager there was no excuse for allowing them to still have control over my life and my future. Thinking about my experiences in school made me mad. I decided that if I was going to fight against the negative views that were held of me as a child I would have to take control of my life as a youth.

People always tell stories about how going to jail has a way of changing a person. I actually started thinking that the encounter with my shady co-worker was a blessing in disguise. The experience forced me to sit down and reevaluate the people who I called my friends. I had walked away from people who wanted to be my true friends and chose to hang out with people who couldn't have cared less about me or my life. I decided in that moment to stop running from people who wanted to help me and open up my heart again.

Many of the ex-felons who had been released from jail had tried to talk to me and my boys about not making the same mistakes they did. They told us that being locked up changes you. I observed this fact in movies like *Malcolm X* and *The Hurricane*. I never imagined that *I* would be in the position these ex-felons were in until I saw those cell doors close.

I would never liken my experience in jail to those ex- felons or someone like Malcolm X, but I know this from experience: hearing a jail cell slam closed and realizing that you are no longer free to make decisions for yourself will force you to stop running around and sit down and think about making changes in your life.

I laid on the bunk thinking about my life in East Texas. How I used to sat out on the porch and just stare up at the stars and wonder what was out there.

Lessons in the Jail Cell

It had been years since I had really thought about the conversations with my Grandfather. But sitting in that jail cell I started thinking about all of the lessons I had learned on the farm. This is where I *really* learned how to be a competitor and chase down the things that I wanted, just like the chickens. I thought of how I would run as fast as I could to get away from the wasps. It seemed like ever since I could remember I had just been running away from things. I had never even taken time to stop and think. For the first time since I was a kid I had stopped running.

In this moment I was reminded of who I was. I was a competitor. I had always risen to the challenges that life brought my way when I was a child.

Everything that people tried to tell me made sense now. When I was in the 8th grade, my football coach saw that I was struggling with school and doing the right thing. He pulled me to the side one day and asked me a question which didn't sink in until now. Now that I was forced to sit down and think about it.

My coach said, "Joseph, if someone came up to you and punched you in the face what would you do? Would you fight back?"

I responded, "Yeah coach, I ain't no punk."

He replied, "You'll fight anyone who gets in your way. You'll defend yourself if someone punches you in your face?"

I emphasized, "Yeah coach, I'm not crazy. I'm not just going to let somebody punch me in my face and not do anything!"

He sat there for a moment and then looked me in the eye, "Then why is it that when life's challenges punch you in the face you won't fight back? Why is it that when the challenge of doing your school work or staying out of trouble punches you in your face you won't fight back? If you're not a punk then why are you punking out? You have to treat every aspect of your life like it's a challenge."

I now understood what he was trying to teach me. He wanted me to understand that I should use all of the competitiveness and fight that I had inside of me, not only to compete in sports, but also to compete in life.

I sat there and thought about the fact that most of the problems I had gotten myself into were my on doing. I always found myself surrounded by negativity because I was planting seeds of negativity.

My grandfather and coach had taught me many lessons through their stories of survival. It took going to jail to realize that these were stories to help me survive.

Free!

When I first got to jail I was hardened by living on the streets, so crying was something that I wouldn't do. Plus, as the youngest person there, I was not about to cry in front of these grown men. When my mama came to see me, I could see the tears in her eyes. I was heartbroken. I knew that I had let her and everybody that had ever believed in me down. Although I had disappointed her and broken her heart my mother still showed up everyday and cried.

My mother has always been a praying woman and a woman of extreme faith. So one day she showed up and sat in the lobby of the jail and started praying because she didn't have the money to bail me out. As fate and her faith would have it, I was praying in my jail cell at the same time, vowing to change my life. Our prayers were answered. As she sat there in that lobby she heard a man's voice telling the clerk that he was there to bail out a kid named Joseph Mathews.

Words cannot explain the joy I felt when the bailiff came to the cell and called my name and said, "You're going home." I jumped up, took off that orange jump suit, put my clothes back on, looked at all of the other people who were sitting around sad, broken, and institutionalized and walked out of the cell down the long hallway.

It was a strange feeling because as I walked down the hallway I thought about all of people who had walked down this same hallway to freedom only to return because they had prayed and made promises but hadn't truly made up their minds to change.

I had no clue who came to bail me out. I walked into the lobby and saw my mother standing there with tears in her eyes and then I saw my friend Chris's dad. He had heard that I was in jail and came to bail me out.   He knew I had potential and didn't want to see it wasted behind bars. He also knew that's what his late son Chris would've wanted. I walked out of that jail and made up my mind that I would not be coming back. I was going to do just what the bailiff said. I was going home...

Chapter 14
Rehab

The day I walked out of jail was the greatest and scariest day of my life. It's easy to say what you're going to do when you're locked up, but now that I was free to make decisions for myself again, the temptation of going back to the streets were very strong. I literally got headaches because of the stress that built up sitting around my mother's house.

I didn't tell any of my friends that I was back from jail because I knew they would come by asking me to go hang. I knew that if I was going to make the change I said I wanted to make while in jail, I would have to stay away from the people who helped me to go there.

It had been almost a year since Chris's death and since Joey and I had spoken. Just as I started to get lonely and contemplate going back to the streets, Joey showed up at my house. It turns out that he was the one who called Chris's dad trying to raise money to get me out.

We sat in my room talking and it felt just like old times again. We talked about sports, girls, and music. He asked me what I was going to do with my life. It had been a long time since anyone had talked to me about my life and following my dreams. I probably wouldn't have wanted to hear it from anybody except Joey because he truly knew me and I trusted him.

I asked him about all of my old teammates. He told me something that truly changed my life. He said that the day Chris died my teammates were crying and hanging their heads. They needed me to help them just as much as I needed their help. They didn't come to my school just to console me. They were looking to me for leadership. It wasn't only his idea to come and see me. Joey expressed to me that my teammates had always looked up to me because they knew that I had had it rough but I still was able to lead them and make them believe. They had always wanted to be there for me but they just didn't know how.

Hearing this helped me understand that the leadership abilities I possessed that my peers had been drawn to as a kid hadn't left me like I once suspected. I had needed to hear this all along.

I really didn't know what to say because I felt so bad that I'd left him and Chris hanging. I started to apologize to him but as soon as I started, he stopped me and said, "I have an even better idea than you apologizing to me. I want you come back to school. It's time for you to come back home. Let's finish up together. That's what Chris would want because he believed in you more than anybody. That's what I want because I believe in you too."

I knew he was not going to let me tell him no, so I agreed to come back and try to finish school. After being out for a year, living in the streets, and going to jail, I was on my way back to school to finish. I knew that it wouldn't be easy, but I was determined.

But the real test would be proving to my doubters and haters that I was determined.

Chapter 15
Back to School

One of the last things Joey said when he left that day was that I was not alone and that he was going to be there for me. The next day his daddy helped me get enrolled in school. The day after that Joey pulled up in my driveway and honked his horn. It was a Tuesday one week after our senior year had started.

We pulled up to the school and I just sat there for a few minutes. I had butterflies in my stomach. I looked over at Joey and said, "Man this is crazy. My schoolboy days are over. I've been to jail, I've been running the streets, I've seen people get shot and I haven't done homework in years."

Joey looked at me and started laughing. He said, "Yeah ain't that crazy? But man, you're going to make it." So I got out of the car and walked into the school with my boy Joey by my side. The high school dropout had returned.

I had been preparing for the initial shock of going back to school. I was prepared for the fact that people were going to react when they saw me, but you can never be fully prepared.

When I walked into the school it was like a movie. You know the scene where the person walks in and the music stops and people stop talking and just stare. Although there wasn't any music playing, that's how it felt.

At first, people didn't know what to say, but after the initial shock of seeing me, everybody came up and welcomed me back. Being welcomed back by my peers wasn't that hard. I had to answer a lot of questions like, "Why did you leave? Where have you been? Why did you come back?" but overall it was okay.

It was the response from my teachers which let me know that I had something to prove. When they laid eyes on me it was like they had just seen a ghost. I guess I can see why they looked at me like I was a ghost, because to them, statistically I was dead. They had seen so many kids drop out of school, but they had only seen a few come back, especially a student like me.

I really couldn't blame them for looking at me like I was crazy. I hadn't been a good student throughout high school so when they saw me walk back through those school doors they thought they were going to have to put up with the same old Joseph. They had no idea what I had been through in the past year. The truth is they had no clue what I had been through all of my life. If they had, they would have understood why I had the heart to walk back in that school, even though most of them didn't believe in me. It was okay because I was a totally different person. I believed in myself again.

Chapter 16
Learning from My M.C.'s

At one time, school was very uncomfortable for me but after being in jail and out on the street, I was as comfortable as I could get. That made all of the difference in the world. My 3rd grade year made me so uncomfortable with reading and writing, to the point that I would just sit there and do nothing. Throughout high school I hadn't gotten over my academic insecurity.

When I first returned to class, I remember my English teacher handing me my book. I opened it, and to my surprise I could still read. I was a little rusty but I could read.

That was all I needed to boost my confidence. After that I knew it was on. I started reading anything I could get my hands on.

Hip Hop became huge in the 90's, and many of the people who inspired me when I was out there in the streets were rappers like Biggie, 2pac, Nas, Common and many others. I knew that as hard as some of them were and as hard as some of them acted, they all had one thing in common. They all had an extensive vocabulary which didn't come from just being on the streets. It came from them reading a lot of books and newspapers and writing a lot too.

Whenever me and my boys listened to Tupac they always listened to the side of him that was a thug like we were; but when I listened to him I heard the side of him that was hurting as he rapped about the painful things he had experienced, witnessed and read about. That motivated me to read even more because I knew that one day I wanted to work to change some of things that these artists rapped about. I was now 18 years old and hadn't been in an honors class since I was 8 but my hunger for learning was back.

The Return of the Champion

One of the realities that I had to deal with when I came back to school was that I had been out for a year. That meant I had a lot of credits to make up in order to graduate. If I wanted to graduate on time I would have to go to credit recovery night school for the entire year and then go to summer school all summer.

I didn't even want to think about the long road I had In front of me to graduate so I rejoined the football team. Many colleges around the country were once interested in me playing football for them, but moving around a lot and dropping out of school resulted in most of those opportunities drying up, but I couldn't let that get me down. I had to keep going.

When I was a sophomore me and my team won the state championship in wrestling. So I decided to go back out for the team as a senior. I won another State Championship at the 178 weight class my career high school record ended up being 90 wins and only 5 loses.

People were so surprised that I came back out of nowhere and won the State Championship in wrestling again. They failed to realize that I had been wrestling all of my life, with life. I had been wrestling with growing up poor, growing up in a broken family, being an angry kid, running the streets as a teenager, and going to jail. Now I was wrestling with the new and evolving person I was becoming and there was no one out there who was a tougher challenge to me than I was to myself.

Chapter 17
Night School

Night school was tough. I went to school all day, practiced in the evening, and went to school at night. Looking back on it, all of the extra work was helping me become a better student. Even though I was working really hard, a lot of people around me still didn't believe in me.

Because of my past experiences, I had never had a great relationship with the police; so it's very ironic that a police officer ended up being the one who lit the fire in me that got me through the long hours of night school.

I had just started going to night school and one evening the on-duty police officer pulled me to the side and said, "Hey Joseph, you don't know me but I want to tell you something. I was in the lounge the other day and overheard some teachers talking about you. They were betting that you won't even make it out of night school let alone graduate."

Were there really teachers willing to bet that I was going fail? He looked me in the eye and said, "Man I've watched you compete for a long time and I believe that you have what it takes. I'm pulling for you and I want you to prove them wrong."

His words encouraged me not to give up. To this day I wish I could find that man because he brought that classroom competitor that was once inside of me back to life. It was like God sent him just in time because he knew that I was about to be tested.

As the time drew closer to graduation we all took senior pictures, but when the year books came out I was nowhere to be found in it. I guess the teacher who was over the year book didn't think I had what it took to graduate either so he didn't even bother putting my picture in the book. Although I wasn't happy I still had to keep going.

Be All You Can Be

The principal of the school had been there for a while and had seen me in his office quite a few times, so when he called me to his office one day I thought I'd done something wrong. When I walked in his office there was a military recruiter sitting with him. He asked me to sit down.

The principal told me how proud he was of me for coming back to school, but said he was concerned about me because he didn't think that I was going to make it out of there. He told me he wanted to make a deal with me. It was March, and if I signed up to go to the Marines right then and there he would let me graduate and I wouldn't even have to finish out the year. I guess he felt like he was doing me a favor. All he did was made me that much more determined to graduate. I don't know what more they wanted from me. I came back to school, I was doing my homework, I was staying out of trouble, and I was going to night school and people still didn't believe in me.

"Mama, I'm Going to Graduate"

Although I still needed 2 semesters of summer school, all I needed in order to walk across the stage at graduation was a passing grade in my final night school class.

I remember the last night of school like it was yesterday. All that day at school I was walking around nervous. All day long I had teachers and classmates asking me, "Well, do you think you made it?" I was as honest as I could be and replied, "Yeah, I believe so." But Truthfully, I was a little uneasy because it's one thing to be in control of an outcome, but when other people are in control I get a little nervous. Since the 3rd grade, my experiences with teachers had been so bad that I really didn't trust any of them to do the right thing.

I made sure that I handled my part of the deal. That night I walked into the classroom and the teacher handed me my grade. When I saw that I had passed I felt like I was floating on a cloud. I wanted to cry, scream, and get up and leave to tell my mama, but we were given our grades at the beginning of class so I had to wait. I couldn't even call her during the break because we didn't have a home phone, so I just sat there in a trance.

Later on that night when I saw my mother I got to tell her something that I never even imagined that I would get to say to her. I hugged her tight and said, "Mama I'm going to graduate."

Cap and Gown

Because the school was not sure if I would make it through a year of night school and regular school, I wasn't initially allowed to file for graduation. The day after I received my grades and two days before graduation I walked into the office to file for graduation and pick up my cap and gown. I remember telling the secretary why I was there. And she looked at me like, "Yeah right." She checked, doubled-checked, and then made about two more calls. She couldn't believe that I was going to be walking across the stage. She looked like she had just lost a bet!

As she was checking I just stood there patiently. I had learned that sometimes when people can't stop you from rising, they will try to create environments that will cause you to trip and fall. She couldn't and didn't want to believe that I was going to graduate, so she was purposely giving me a hard time, thinking that I would go off on her. When that happened I would get into trouble, and not be allowed to graduate. She didn't realize that I was no longer the Joseph she once thought she knew. I had conquered my internal battle of not controlling my attitude. I had learned not to let small things make me angry. There was nothing she could do to me that was going to make me mess up what I had worked hard for.

Besides, there was no need to trip because I knew I was right. So I stood there and watched the secretary walk over to the closet, open the door and grab *my* red cap and gown. She walked over to me, put those precious garments in my hand and said, "Here you go." I just stood there looking down at them. I thought about how I had seen all the other kids walking down the hallway with their caps and gowns. I always wondered how I would feel when I was holding mine. Now that I had it, I felt better than I could have imaged.

Chapter 18
Graduation Day

The morning of graduation I opened up my eyes and just stared up at the ceiling. My whole life flashed before my eyes. I thought about how I used to lay down in my bed at the house on the farm in East Texas and stare up at the sky wondering what was out in the world. It had only been twelve years later and I had not only found out what was out there, but I had seen the worst of what this world has to offer.

When I was running the streets, I thought about death all the time because that's what I saw everyday in my neighborhood. Whether

I was seeing people who were broken from years of living in poverty or suffering from drug addiction, or attending many of my friend's funerals. I just knew that I was going to die at an early age so I was I living my life as though I was already dead.

For the first time since 2nd grade I wasn't thinking about dying anymore. I was thinking about living and all of the possibilities that were waiting for me in the future. My future was something that I hadn't even taken time to think about. In spite of all I'd been through, I was grateful to still be alive because as long I was alive, there was hope and a purpose for my life.

I Made It!

It was 5:00 p.m. and graduation was going to take place in two hours. I pulled my cap and gown out of the closet. When I received it I didn't even take it out of the bag. I wanted the experience to feel like I was opening a present on a special day.

I put on the shirt and slacks that my church had given me and then opened that bag and put my cap and gown on for the first time. I stood there looking at myself in the mirror for a long time.

Less than a year ago I was a high school drop out lying in a jail cell. Although my grades were only better than three people in my entire graduation class, being ranked 163rd out of 166 graduates was fine with me. I was graduating and that's all that mattered.

My Time to Shine

It was 6:15 p.m., and just like my first day back to school, my homeboy Joey pulled into my driveway and I got into his car. We just looked at each other and started laughing. We were thinking the same thing. He put his hand on my shoulder and said, "Man I told you that you were going to make it." That's all I needed to hear.

At graduation, Joey and I were seated next to each other because our last names were close. That was just how it should have been. He was the main reason I was there. During graduation, different speakers got up to speak. We just sat there impatiently waiting to get to the part of the ceremony when they called our names and we walked across the stage.

When the time finally came, the program took an unexpected turn. They brought our friend Chris's family to the stage and told them that although he wasn't there, they wanted them to know that they wished he were and that he was still part of the family.

Joey and I hadn't talked much about Chris not being with us at graduation, but we both knew that although it was a special day something was missing. Our friend who we had grown up with, talked about life with, and who had made us laugh was not there to walk across the stage into our future. His family stood there on stage receiving Chris's diploma and Joey and I both broke down crying.

A Lesson about Gambling

One of the interesting things about graduations is that during the ceremony all of the teachers and counselors sit on the stage while the principal shakes all of the graduate's hands as he gives them their diploma.

When they started calling our names I watched my classmates walk across the stage and shake the principal's hand as their families cheered and clapped. As my time drew closer, I wondered how he would respond when he saw me. What would he think about his offer to allow me to graduate in exchange for signing up with the military because he thought I didn't have what it took to make it?

I looked at all of the teachers sitting on the stage. These were the same teachers who had looked at me like I was ghost when

I returned to school. I wondered which ones had bet against me.

They called Joey's name first. He turned around, looked at me and started laughing, and then he walked onto the stage.

Out of the corner of my eye I could see my mother smiling from ear to ear and then they called my name. My grandfather always taught me to look people in the eye so I walked onto the stage and looked the principal in the eye. I could tell he was shocked.

As a kid, I always dreamt of becoming a teacher, but my 3rd grade teacher temporarily assassinated that dream. I was finally back from the dead to teach her and everyone that had ever doubted me that they were wrong.

I looked in the eyes of my teachers. Many of them were speechless. A few even had tears running down their faces. My teachers, my peers, the thousands of people in attendance, and most importantly myself, had been taught a valuable life lesson; you should never give up on or count out someone with a dream. So I guess I became a teacher that day.

As I walked off of the stage my best friend who had saved my life, the friend who had talked me into coming back to school, was waiting for me when I walked off that stage. Joey never admitted it but he was probably more emotional than I was because he knew what I had been through. In spite of everything that I went through - even when it seemed as if everybody else doubted - he never stopped believing in me.

The Final Goodbye to My Friend

The Sunday after graduation Joey and I attended our friend Chris's church for a special ceremony in his honor. His family asked us to come to the pulpit and speak about Chris. We used to hang out at his church all the time in Junior High, and his church was there for us when he died. Being back there was like coming back home.

After service, as we were saying goodbye to everyone, Chris's father came up and hugged us like he never wanted to let us go. It had been a year since his only son had died and he was still heartbroken. Seeing Joey and I together again brought back bittersweet memories. Joey, Chris's father, and I all shared a moment that day. We had all been putting up this front, pretending that we were too tough to cry around each other. That day, we finally came together and cried. It wasn't until then that we were finally ready let go and say goodbye to Chris. We had to do this if we were going to go out and live our lives.

At the time we didn't know we'd soon return to that church with heavy hearts to say goodbye once again.

Saying Goodbye

It had been a week since graduation. I had some serious decisions to make about my life. I didn't go through all of the things I had been through to just go back and hang out in the hood. Joey had enlisted in the Air Force and was scheduled to leave the Wednesday after graduation. We hung out for a few days, embraced and then he left for basic training,

Chris's dad was already in the Air Force. After the car crash he couldn't stand being in Oklahoma any longer, so he took a job with the Pentagon in Washington, DC.

College Bound

What I did next was unbelievable. I accepted a scholarship offer to go out of town and play college football. That's right, I said *college*. How in the world could someone who went through as much as I had just trying to get out of high school even think about going to college?

Until the day I left for college, I had no clue where my life was headed. All I knew is that as a kid I always had these dreams of doing something with my life, and if I was ever going to make those dreams come true, I needed to leave for a while to become whatever I was supposed to be.

The morning I left my mama and my stepfather, the man who became my dad in many ways, stood at the door. My older brothers loaded my things into the car and she just looked at me. I knew in her heart that she didn't want to see her youngest son leave, but there was nothing around there for me but trouble. This was the best thing for my future and my safety. Plus, she knew there was something out there for me to do.

She hugged me and I kissed her on her forehead like I had always done and then got into my brothers car. Once again, I felt like I did when I was a kid and my family loaded up and left the place we called home to move to Oklahoma City where I had no clue what was waiting for me. My brother and I got in the car and headed down the street. I looked out of the window and thought about how I used to run and play up and down these streets with my homies. We were all poor and didn't have much but we always found a way to laugh like the innocent kids we were. Little did we know that one day these same streets would be the place where we'd lose our innocence, lose our dreams and many of us would even lose our lives.

The irony was that now that look of pain and suffering in the eyes of the young kids who were now walking the streets would be my motivation to get through the difficult times ahead of me in college. I knew that one day I would be back to save them and help them live their dreams. But first, I had to leave to go pursue my own.

Chapter 19
College

I was entering my third year of college. It was officially my junior year. Don't get me wrong, I had my struggles because I started college academically behind, but by now I had learned how to use my street smarts to help me with my class work.

While in college I continued to play football, wrestle, and run track. Those sports took me all over the country, and eventually the world.

The thing that I loved most about college was the people I met from all over. When I was younger I used to read about all of these interesting places and now I was at school with people who were from these places.

I was even the co-founder of a campus chapter of the Civil Rights organization that my grandfather used to have me read about – The National Association for the Advancement of Colored People (N.A.A.C.P.) on my college campus. During football season I was voted Homecoming King.

Even though I left behind many things from my past, being able to attract pretty girls wasn't one of them, and it finally paid off. I dated and eventually married a sorority girl who was also the campus queen. She was graduating that spring and I was going the graduate the following spring.

The Only One Left

My life seemed to be going pretty well, but I was going to be hurt severely one more time. My girl and I had just returned to her apartment after watching a movie. When we went into the house, her roommates told me that a lot of my friends and family members from Oklahoma City had been trying to reach me all day. They gave me a number to call. At first I thought it was one of my old classmates wanting to get tickets to come watch a football game or something, but when I called the number back, it was Joey's brother.

He called to tell me that my best friend Joey had just committed suicide in Tampa, Florida where he was living. We had just talked two weeks earlier because he was getting married. I was supposed to be his best man and planning his bachelor party. Now his brother was on the phone telling me that my best friend - the only person who had been there for me during the most difficult times in my life, the one who was solely responsible for me going back to high school, was gone.

I had never felt worse in my life. The day was April 21st. I packed up a few things and left for home as fast as I could. In a three year span I had come home a hand full of times to go to a homeboy's funeral, but I never imagined that I would have to come back for my 21 year old best friend's funeral.

Joey's father was the one who took me to get re-enrolled in high school. He always made sure that I was taken care of while I was in high school. The one thing that was going to hurt me the most was the thing that he needed me to do. He needed me to come and be with the family while they prepared for his funeral. I couldn't say no.

I can't imagine anything more heartbreaking than being in the home of a parent who has just lost a child. Everyday, I watched them lay there and cry. A few times, people came by and they tried to be strong, but they were more heartbroken than anyone I'd ever seen.

Joey's dad was always so strong, but now he was as weak as a person could get. When he came and sat down beside me and asked me if I would be the speaker for Joey's funeral I couldn't say no.

The family and I woke up the morning of the funeral and Joey's mother and father just took turns breaking down crying because the reality that they were getting ready to bury their son was setting in.

Joey's dad asked everyone to come together and then he asked me to pray for the family. To this day I don't know why he asked me to pray because I definitely was not a preacher, but I stood there and prayed for the family. We got into the limousine and headed to the funeral.

During all of the craziness of the week I never stopped to ask where the services were going to be held. My heart was heavy when I realized that we were pulling up to Chris's church. This was the same place that we had hung out at as kids and this was the last time we would be together.

It had only been three short years since Joey and I were asked to stand at the podium to speak about Chris. And now here I was now standing alone, speaking about my best friend Joey. I looked down at the large crowd of people who were hurting and in need of comfort and direction. I couldn't help but reflect back on the dreams I had as a kid about standing at a podium speaking in front of a crowd.

Until then, I had been a shy person and I was hesitant to stand in front of people, but when I looked down at my friend lying in that casket I realized right then that he knew he had a mission. That was the reason he always spoke such positive things into my life even when everything around me was negative. His mission was to save me.

He was the one who made me feel smart in junior high when no one else thought I was smart. He got me bailed out of jail and talked me into coming back to school. If he hadn't come to my house and asked me to come back to school when he did, I probably would have ended up committing suicide too. He was only in my life for a season, but he did what he was supposed to do for me. I thank him love him and dedicate this book to his memory.

The morning of the funeral, rain was falling from the sky just like the day when I was a heartbroken 6 year old saying goodbye to my home. Maybe the rain really *is* God and all of the angels in heaven crying for the kids who are hurting on earth, because that day, I cried more than I had in my entire life.

Chapter 20
Epilogue

Not a day has passed since Joey's death that I haven't thought about him, but after the funeral I knew exactly what I was supposed to do in order to honor my friend for saving my life.

The next year when they called my name at college graduation, I looked back and started laughing, just like Joey had done at our high school graduation. In my heart, I knew he was there. God knows I wish that Joey and Chris could have been there in person to see me graduating from college, but when I walked across that stage I carried their spirits with me.

After the ceremony, I sat proudly in my seat while my mother snapped pictures with a big "cheesy" smile on her face. Little did she know that one of those pictures would one day be printed on the back of my first book – so you can thank her for my beautiful college graduation picture.

Special Education Again

After graduating from college I eventually went on to play professional football in Europe and even traveled to Africa - the place that my grandfather always talked to me about, but never got a chance to visit. But out all of the experiences that I've had, nothing has been more rewarding and fulfilling to me than the day I walked down a long hallway into a classroom in Dallas, TX, and stood at a podium, and introduced myself as the new Special Education teacher.

Now I stand at podiums around the country as a youth motivational speaker and on Sundays I deliver sermons as a youth minister, encouraging young people to make better choices in their lives and pursue the dreams that they have in their hearts. I have even made many television appearances around the country.

Remember how I used to stare at the big buildings in Oklahoma City when I was 6 years old and wonder what the people inside the State Capitol did for a living? In 2007 when the crime and violence began to break out on the streets of Oklahoma City, the news stations and all those rich and important people in those big buildings across the street called on me for assistance.

My family and I had lived right across the street from the Capitol without food to eat and we slept without furniture on the cold hardwood floor. Ironically, the very people I used to wonder about were in need of my help. Many of them had neither the experience nor the knowledge that it would take to understand and make a difference in the lives of troubled youth. Because of my life experiences, I did.

I stood at that podium on the floor of the State Senate in Oklahoma City, and spoke in order to help bring awareness to all of those leaders about young people's issues. I drew from my own experiences and spoke about the solutions that would be needed in order to give youth the help they need to stay off the streets and out of trouble. As a result of that speech, over a million dollars was spent on programs that will help kids get jobs instead of locking up every kid who is troubled or in a gang. There are now fun programs for kids to be a part of that will help keep them off the streets and out of gangs.

A couple of months after losing their little old home that had been falling apart, to a fire, my mother and stepfather were on local and national television because a brand new home was being built for them by an organization that helps people who have experienced tragedies. I told you my mama was a praying woman!

Chasing Down a Dream

The road was tough and there were many nights that I wondered if I would make it, but I never gave up. I held on to my dream and as a result I went from being a high school dropout to living out my life long dream of becoming a high school teacher. When I started my career as a high school teacher it had been 15 years since we'd moved from East Texas to Oklahoma City. In those years, my family lived in an empty apartment with no food to eat, spent many days with no water to drink, and many nights without electricity to see, but I made it. I went from being a straight A student to being thrown into Special Education classes to die, but I survived that too.

I overcame the self-destructive path that I was on when I went to jail and dropped out of school by making up my mind that I was better than how I was living. I went back to school and did the unthinkable. I went on to college and became the first one in my family and my neighborhood to graduate from college.

I often think back to the day that I left for college. It was tough leaving my neighborhood. I couldn't help looking back and wondering, "Why me? Why was I allowed to make it out when so many of my homies didn't?" I believe that one of the reasons is because I ultimately made up my mind that I wanted to do something with my life. I decided the only way that would happen was if I did something different.

The other reason I believe I made it is because there was a purpose for my life even when I dropped out of school and was walking around lost and hurting other people. Deep in my heart I knew that I had a calling to help people. I truly believe that the only reason I survived my childhood and the nightmares that I had to endure was because of the glimpses of my future that I would see in my mind and my dreams; a future of speaking to, encouraging, and helping to heal hurting people one day.

During the storms, the ups and downs, and the pain and suffering - even when it seemed as if I had nothing - it seemed like that dream always came back into my mind and told me not to give up. It was almost like it would speak directly to my heart and say, "Keep chasing me just like you used to chase those chickens on the farm. Keep chasing me because people are hungry and if you give up on chasing me then you'll not only starve, but other people will starve as well."

I really didn't realize it then, but when I was back on the farm chasing chickens and fishing it was never just about me. It was about others as well. If I didn't do what I was supposed to do, other people would suffer because of it. Often, we take in the lessons and experiences from the pain and suffering we go through and hold on to them as if we own them, but the truth is, we don't.

We should all remember that the hardships, pain, and suffering that we go through teach us lessons and we are supposed to take what we learn and help other people who we see hurting, struggling or in need of direction. It's a part of the cycle of life.

When I look back on my life, I know that if I'm not a hero to anyone else, I am a hero to myself. I have risen to and conquered every challenge that has come my way. Every attempt that was made to enslave me I have fought through to set my self free.

In a way, I see myself like the abolitionist Frederick Douglas who was once a slave but learned how to read and freed himself so he could one day return to help free others because that's what I do as a teacher. I fight to free the minds of my students so they can live their dreams and be free.

Many kids who are going through drama in their lives often ask me, "Man what's up with this? Why is all this happening to me?"

I tell them the truth. If you are a person who's always going through a lot of drama, it's because you're being prepared to be a hero for someone else one day. Your life is preparing you to be a testimony for youth who are coming along after you. You already know some of the kids that you're going to inspire. They're your younger family members – your little brothers, sisters, nephews, nieces, and cousins; but you haven't even met most of the kids who are going to be looking up to you, because they are in elementary school or they haven't even been born yet. But they're going to be looking to you for inspiration and guidance one day. They need you to step up and fight against life's challenges and be a champion to yourself so you can one day be a champion for them.

The question is: Are they worth it, and do you accept the challenge?

Discussion Guide

Chapter 1

1. Although I got away from the wasps, making them angry could have been very dangerous. Is there anything that you play around with that could be dangerous?

2. When I was a little kid on my family farm, I chased chickens. What are you chasing in life?

3. What lessons did I learn from my days on my grandfather's farm?

4. Who in your life can you go to and ask questions about your family's history?

5. How do you think my life would have turned out if I had not known my family history?

6. What are some of the other lessons from you learned from Chapter 1?

Chapter 2

1. When my family moved from the country to the city it was very hard for me to adjust. How do you adjust to changes in your life?

2. Many nights we went to bed hungry, or had very little to eat. Do you ever find yourself wasting food or water that other kids would love to have?

3. My mother worked as hard as she could for us when other people chose to leave. Do you appreciate the people in your life who have chosen to stay?

4. When I was six years old I developed a business plan to make money. Can you think of any "legal" business ideas that you and your friends can implement?

5. When I saw the people in my community hurting I was heartbroken and wanted to do something about it. How do you feel when you see people hurting in your community? What can you do to make a difference?

6. At a young age I knew that I was a smart leader. What are some of the talents and gifts that you possess?

7. What are some of the other lessons from that you learned from Chapter 2?

Chapter 3

1. As a kid I read a lot of books about people I looked up to. Can you think of anyone you look up to that you would like to read about?

2. When I was younger I always loved helping my peers with their class work. When you see your peers struggling with class work what do you do?

3. Getting out of poverty was my main motivation to stay focused and do well in school. What is your motivation to stay focused?

4. The people I hung out with in 2nd grade helped me to become a better student. How do the people that you hang out with at school help you to become better?

5. What are some of the other lessons from that you learned from Chapter 3?

Chapter 4

1. In 2nd grade, when I was having conflict with my teacher, what do you think I should have done?

2. During the conflict with my teacher I never said anything to my mother. Was that a good decision? What should I have done?

3. Even though I felt like my teacher was treating me unfairly, what are some of the things that I could have done differently?

4. Can you think of any people that you can go to for help if what happened to me ever happened to you or someone you love.

5. What are some of the other lessons from that you learned from Chapter 4?

Chapter 5

1. After my ordeal in 3rd grade I felt like a bird that was being kept from flying. Is there anything in your heart that you're not doing, but feel like you should be doing?

2. In Chapter 5, I use the quote "hurt people, hurt people." Do you ever find yourself hurting people physically or emotionally because you're hurting?

3. I never got a chance to apologize to the kids that I hurt. Can you think of anybody that you hurt and should apologize to?

4. What are some of the other lessons from that you learned from Chapter 5?

Chapter 6

1. In chapter 6 I revealed that I had a reputation for being a bully. What is your reputation?

2. If you or someone you know was being bullied, what would you do?

3. Wrestling helped me to channel some of my built up frustrations.   Is there anything you can do, to channel your built up frustrations positively?

4. One of the mistakes that I made when I started playing sports was seeking attention because of my low self esteem. What are some of the things that you and other people do to seek attention?

5. What are some of the other lessons from that you learned from Chapter 6?

Chapter 7

1. When I started junior high school I prejudged and was distrustful of all white people because of my experience with my 3rd grade teacher. Have you ever prejudged people you didn't know because of past experiences?

2. If I had let that bitterness last when I met Joey and Chris would we have become best friends?

3. Where do you think I would have ended up if I hadn't met Joey and Chris?

4. What are some of the other lessons from that you learned from Chapter 7?

Chapter 8

1. Many of the people around me viewed me as a dumb athlete, and that's how I began to behave. Do you act the way people view you?

2. In high school people thought that I was dumb and not able to read. These were hurtful and untrue rumors. How do you feel and respond when someone spreads untrue rumors about you?

3. There were a lot of people smiling in my face as if they loved me, but they were hating on me behind my back. Do you listen to gossip about other people? If so, what does that say about you?

4. What are some of the other lessons from that you learned from Chapter 8?

Chapter 9

1. Going to the big school across town but living in the "hood" made me feel torn because I was living in two worlds. Do you ever feel torn between two worlds? If so, how do you handle it?

2. Growing up in my old neighborhood, everybody only talked about the negative aspects of our community. Is there anything positive that you can find, and talk about in your community?

3. When the movie *Colors* came out in the early 90's, people who lived in the same neighborhood became enemies overnight just because of what they saw in a movie. How do you allow movies to affect you and the decisions you make?

4. Most of my friends who joined gangs ended up either dead or in jail. If you knew where you were headed and where you were going to end up, how would that effect your decision to join a group that was up to no good?

5. What are some of the other lessons from that you learned from Chapter 9?

Chapter 10

1. When I left my old school it seemed like the same problems followed me. Does it seem as if everywhere you go the same problems follow you? Do you think that some of the drama you go through is of your own making?

2. One of the things that I regret the most is that when I was depressed as a youth, I always tried to handle everything on my own and never talked to a counselor. Do you ever feel depressed? Who do you talk to about it?

3. When my friend Chris died, my friend Joey was there for me when I needed him the most. Do you have friends that will be there for you when you need them the most? Are you the type of friend who will be there for your friends when they need you?

4. What are some of the other lessons from that you learned from Chapter 10?

1. In this chapter, I wrote about how I allowed all of the negative things I had been through to control my life. Do you pay more attention to the positive or negative events in your life? Which ones do you allow to control you?

2. My boy Jimmy and I were never officially in a gang but we always hung tight with them. Do you ever "hang around" negative people or things that you are not necessarily an official part of? How could this potentially affect your future?

3. If we were hanging with a gang when something went down, would it have mattered if we were not officially in the gang?

4. When my homeboy Jimmy was asked to get in the car and ride with those gang members, he truly didn't want to go. What do you think they would have done, if he had said no?

5. If someone is planning on doing dirt that could put their lives or freedom at risk, are they your true friends if they want

you to join them even though they know that you could be killed or go to jail?

6. Having the courage to say no can be tough. If Jimmy had had the courage to say no would he still be alive? Do you have the courage to say no?

7. When Jimmy was hiding in the back seat of the car while his friends were being shot, I believe he was wishing for another chance. Have you ever been in a bad situation and wished you had another chance?

8. Jimmy had been given chance after chance to change. As soon as he got out of trouble he would go right back to doing the same thing. Does a person who keeps asking for another chance yet continues to do the same things really want to change?

9. My boy Reggie wanted me to sell drugs to little kids in my old neighborhood. How do you feel about people who sell drugs in your neighborhood? How would you feel if it was a young family member who was buying drugs from the neighborhood drug dealer?

10. What are some of the other lessons from that you learned from Chapter 11?

1. Me and my boys used to show up to our friends funerals and watch their mothers cry, then go right back and do what they did to get killed. When we said we loved our mothers were we telling the truth?

2. When I got the job at the clothing store, I was given a lot of responsibility, but I had no intention of being responsible. How do you treat responsibilities that you are given

3. While working at the store I had a chance to be honest but I chose to be dishonest. Are you an honest person? (Be honest!)

4. When my shady co-worker walked into the store and wanted to get the "hook up" I should have known that something was wrong. Do you notice shady people when you meet them? Do you still hangout with them?

5. Although I wasn't the only person taking clothes from the store I ended up taking the fall and going to jail. Have you ever taken the rap for something that others shared responsibility in?

6. What are some of the other lessons from that you learned from Chapter 12?

Chapter 13

1. While I was lying on the bunk in jail, I realized that I had been setting myself up to be a statistic. What are you setting yourself up for?

2. While in jail I thought about all of the people who had tried to talk some sense into me and my boys and how we were not trying to hear it. Has anyone ever tried to talk to you about making the right decisions? Did you listen?

3. My coach asked me why I wouldn't rise to the challenge and fight against life's temptations, the same way I'd fight if someone punched me in the face. What challenges do you need to rise up and fight against?

4. When I was in jail I was forced to watch my mother cry because I had broken her heart. Whose heart would you break if you get into trouble?

5. When I got out of jail, my friend Joey was the friend who checked on me. Who has been there for you when you were in trouble?

6. What are some of the other lessons from that you learned from Chapter 13?

Chapter 14

1. When I got out of jail I was on probation and couldn't get into any more trouble. If I returned home and started hanging out with the same people what do you think would have eventually happened?

2. Do you have any friends that you left hanging like I left my friends Joey and Chris?

3. Joey came to my house and asked me what I planned on doing with my life. Do you have any friends who will hold you accountable and ask you serious questions about your life?

4. When I dropped out of school I didn't have anybody to talk to before I made that decision. If I had had someone to talk to, do you think I still would have dropped out?

5. When Joey showed up and asked me to come back to school he motivated me to come back. Do you have any friends who are no longer attending school that you could motivate to come back?

6. If Joey had decided not to ask me to come back to school because he didn't think I would listen, would I have come back to school?

7. What are some of the other lessons from that you learned from Chapter 14?

Chapter 15

1. In order for me to come back to school I couldn't be worried about what other people said or thought. How do you respond to what people say and think about you?

2. When the teachers saw me walk back through the doors, they looked at me like they didn't believe in me. How do you respond when people don't believe in you?

3. When I came back to school my friends helped me to not feel lonely and encouraged me until the end. Their encouragement helped me finish. Do you and your friends encourage each other?

4. If I had come back to school and didn't work hard, what would the people who didn't believe in me have said?

5. Who do you let down when you don't give your best effort?

6. What are some of the other lessons from that you learned from Chapter 15?

Chapter 16

1. After I came back to school I began to read any and everything I could get my hands on. Besides this book what is the last book you read. What was it about?

2. In the late 90's the Notorious B.I.G., Tupac, and Nas were some of the M.C.'s who inspired me to read and learn more about the world. What do the rappers and other artists you listen to inspire you to do?

3. When my boys and I listened to Tupac they just wanted to listen to the side of him that rapped about "thug life." They ignored the Tupac who rapped about trying to live a positive life. Do you listen to any rappers who rap about trying to live a positive life?

4. I loved listening to Tupac because I could relate to the pain he had for the poor youth in the "hood". I wanted to come back to my community and help change the things that he rapped about. When you hear someone rap about something that needs to change, are you motivated to make a difference?

5. When I was younger, me and my boys emulated everything our favorite rappers did, said, and wore. We wanted everything they had. When I got older I found out that most of what they had in the music videos was rented! Have you ever tried to act like your favorite rapper?

6. Almost every rapper goes on to be an actor. Is your favorite M.C. a rapper who happens to know how to act or are they just actors who have learned how to act "hard" and "thuggish?

7. Some of the rappers we like, act hard on videos, but after the video shoot they go back to a penthouse. Many youth who have tried to act like them have ended up in the "pen." Are you trying to be like someone who is not real?

8. I was a star athlete but lost almost all of my offers to play sports in college when I dropped out of school. I was very disappointed but I kept on trying. How do you respond to setbacks and disappointments?

9. During my senior year I proved everybody wrong by winning the State Championship in wrestling although no

one thought I would. What are you wrestling with that no one believes you can overcome?

10. Nothing in my life did more damage to me than I did to myself. I was my own worst enemy. What are you to yourself?

11. What are some of the other lessons from that you learned from Chapter 16?

Chapter 17

1. As a youth I had many bad experiences with the police in my neighborhood. Some of it was of my own doing and some of it was harassment. Does the cop at my school telling me not to give up and that he believed in me prove that not all police were out to get me?

2. What would you do if someone you didn't care for gave you really good advice?

3. Even though I never got a chance to say "thank you" to the police officer for believing in me, I wish I could. Do you know anyone that you should thank for believing in you?

4. Even though I was doing all of the right things when I came back to school I still had a lot of nonbelievers. How do you respond to people who always have something negative to say?

5. Even though I had done all I could do on the last day of night school, I was still nervous about my teacher failing me. When you know in your heart that you have done all you can do, should you worry?

6. After all that I had been through, how do you think my mother felt about me telling her I was going to graduate?

7. If you are struggling with school, after all you have been through how do you think that the person who has been taking care of you will feel when you tell them you're going to graduate?

8. When I walked into the office and the secretary didn't want to give me my cap and gown for graduation I really wanted to go off on her. If I had what would have happened?

9. When you know that you're right, do you keep your cool or do you go off?

10. What are some of the other lessons from that you learned from Chapter 17?

Chapter 18

1. The morning of my graduation I woke up and laid in my bed and reflected on the hard work that I had put in to walk across the stage. Do you ever take time to enjoy your accomplishments?

2. Until my senior year I often thought about death and my negative past. What do you spend most of your time thinking about - your past, your present or your future?

3. When I heard that some of the teachers who were sitting on the stage at graduation were betting against me, I got mad and really wanted to say something to them. I chose not to say anything and prove them wrong by graduating. How do you think they felt when they saw me walk across that stage?

4. It took Joey, Chris's dad, and me a whole year before we could really move on with our lives after Chris's death. Have you ever lost a loved one and found yourself having trouble moving on? If so, do you feel like you should talk to someone about it?

5. When I graduated I had no clue what I was going to do with my life. Do you have a plan for your life after graduation and how do you plan on carrying it out?

6. When I decided to go to college I was nervous but I knew that if I was going to do something with my life I would have to leave to become whatever I was supposed to be. Are you willing to leave your current circumstances in order to pursue your dreams?

7. As my brother and I were driving down the street of my neighborhood when I was leaving for college, I looked into the eyes of the kids who were walking around and knew that they would be my motivation to work hard and make it in college. Who or what motivates you to work hard to succeed?

Chapter 19

1. The street smarts that I gained in my old neighborhood were very helpful in getting me through the tough times in college. How do you use your smarts to get through tough times?

2. In college, I met people from all over the world and learned about different cultures which made a better and smarter person. What are some of the other cultures that you know about? How can this knowledge help you be a better person?

3. Growing up, I always had the ability to attract pretty girls. While in college this didn't change, but I did. I found *one girl* and settled down so I could focus on school. How many girls or boys are you focused on?

4. Joey was very good at talking to other people about their problems, but he had trouble talking about his own. Because of this, he ended up committing suicide. Do you ever find yourself being the person who helps everyone else with their problems? Who do you go to in order to talk about your problems?

5. Joey suffered from extreme depression but never told anyone. He ended up breaking the hearts of his family and friends. Do you ever feel extremely depressed? If so, how do you deal with it?

6. What are some of the other lessons from that you learned from Chapter 19?

Chapter 20: Epilogue

1. Have you ever had a dream about what you were going to be in the future?

2. When I graduated from college, I carried the dreams of Joey, Chris, my mother and everyone who ever believed in me with me when I walked across the stage. When you graduate, whose dreams will you carry across the stage with you?

3. After I graduated from college, I returned to the place I struggled with most by becoming a school teacher. What would you like give back to your community?

4. What lessons did you learn from reading this book? How will it help you make better decisions for your life and your future?

Made in the USA
Lexington, KY
29 June 2014